# Alpacas Don't Do That

## Cindy Myers

ISBN-13: 978-1492296447
ISBN-10: 1492296449

www.humsweethum.com

*Acknowledgements*

*I would like to express my appreciation to my amazing sisters, Sally, Hannah, and Ilene for being the very best and most supportive sisters anyone could ask for.*

*Thanks to Sam for being a fantastic proofreader and proving that alpacas help build the best friendships.*

*I'd like to thank Janet for helping me get my intuitive brain kick-started.*

*And most of all, I appreciate the wonderful cast of animals that have so enriched my life.*

# Table of Contents

# Introduction

One of my favorite things to do while visiting my alpacas that I was boarding in Southern California was to sit on the ground under a shelter in the "Maternity" pasture offering gentle energy to the expectant moms. If I kept my energy quiet and non-invasive, they would allow me to share their shelter. There were several hundred alpacas on the ranch, so

*Cindy and Jamilah take a break in the yard.*

they had a single pasture for just the imminently due moms-to-be. At times, there were more than 20 alpacas in that pasture ready to give birth. I knew to sit and intuitively send energy instead of putting my hands on the alpacas. These animals are notorious for being very skittish and dislike being touched. Alpacas are highly instinctual, flight animals. They see us humans as predators so their basic instinct is to be very wary and guarded around us. Those instincts are magnified as they get closer to birthing.

As I sat on the ground, I kept a respectful distance from the dams. I wanted to be as non-threatening as possible. It also helped that I often carried a pouch of their favorite pellet treats. I would sprinkle the pellets on the ground near me, but not so near that the alpacas couldn't easily get away from me if they chose to. Some alpacas were more food motivated and didn't mind taking the treats straight from my hand. It was always their choice if they wanted treats. I wanted to offer comfort. Like any expectant mom, those last days of pregnancy are very uncomfortable. At first they would be quite wary of me, but since I sat on the ground, breathing deeply and sending out this quiet energy, they would go back to what they were doing which was usually grazing on grass, eating hay out of their bins, or cushing (laying down) and resting.

I intuitively would tell the expectant moms that I was offering them gentle energy for any who wished to receive it. I always ask that of an animal because some may not want it and it is a matter of respect to always ask before offering energy. As I'd start my energy session, I'd picture gentle white light entering their bodies. I'd visualize the white light carefully and lightly coursing through their bodies, relaxing them and easing their aches and pains. I'd close my eyes in the beginning to help me picture it better and put myself in a quiet meditative state. But once I had my energy in that quiet mode where my mind was stilled and I was able to focus completely on the energy I was sending, I'd open my eyes to see how it was being experienced and received by the alpacas.

One summer day, five alpacas came towards me. One was Sasha, who was originally imported from the wild alpaca herds in Peru. Imported alpacas are known for being even more skittish than the ones born on our farms and around people from birth. She was probably the most skittish animal at that big farm. She'd scream and pee if you had to catch her. Her instinct was to drop down into what is called a cush position (their legs folded under them while lying down). She was impossible to move in that position. I will never forget the fear in her eyes when we would have to catch her for routine health care activities. But on this warm summer day, with Sasha near term, she came to me voluntarily, just a few feet away to soak up the energy I was offering. This particular fenced area was large but she chose to be near me while I sat sending her energy. She grazed several feet away from me, watching me warily. The other four alpacas were also grazing, some closer to me than Sasha.

I continued to offer the energy and observe how the alpacas, especially Sasha, were accepting it. At one point, I pictured the energy gently going from their heads all the way down to their toes. Spontaneously, all five alpacas that were around me taking up the energy including Sasha, stopped eating and scratched the bottoms of their feet. I had to laugh as I realized my energy accidentally tickled their toes. I didn't mean to do that, but they didn't seem to mind, and continued to enjoy the energy I sent them.

With animals, you often don't know how much they are experiencing from the energy being offered, so when I see a sign like the five alpacas scratching the bottom of their feet the second I pictured sending energy to their toes, I'm excited to receive some validation that it is working. That is probably a human weakness that we seem to need validation. But I admit, I do like it when it happens.

The ability to do energy work with animals has helped me dramatically in my alpaca business. At times my animals do get sick and injured, but having the ability to offer energy to them provides me another tool to give them the best care I can. Because I'm tuned into their energy, I sense when they get sick so I can hopefully head it off before things become more serious. Energy is a tool that provides my animals added comfort and healing opportunities in addition to traditional veterinary care. My energy work has helped me build relationships with animals that are usually skittish around humans. And most of all, this energy work with animals, especially the alpacas, has taught me more about myself. When energy is given, I receive it too. I never fail to learn every time I do energy work on animals. That is the true gift of energy work.

We humans have moved so far away from the intuitive abilities we once depended on for survival. In this American society especially, we are more about output than input. When I worked for the Navy as an Engineer and supervisor, I sat in a meeting with the Captain of the base. He was actually one of the more pleasant and friendlier Captains with more relational abilities than many of the other Captains and managers we had there. He was going over the results of an employee survey taken earlier that year, and like most years, the biggest issue employees had was in the lack of communication they felt they had with managers and leadership. The Captain lectured us supervisors that we had to do better to communicate to the employees what was going on. I knew that wasn't the real issue with the employees. They were frustrated that THEY weren't being listened to. I decided to speak up and make that point. I said that communication really entails two elements. There is the talking piece but there is the other piece that is perhaps even more important, and that is the listening piece of communication. The Captain slammed his hand down on the conference table and said, "You are RIGHT! So next time you are communicating with your employees, make sure they are LISTENING to you!" It wasn't easy, but I stifled the laughter that wanted to burst out of me. Out of the corner of my eye, I saw my boss leaning back in her chair. She had a huge grin on her face. She understood how ridiculous his statement was and that he didn't get the concept that he needed to learn to listen. I have discovered, that the ability for humans to listen, is becoming a lost skill.

Energy work is really about listening. It is not just listening with your ears but listening with all your senses including the intuitive ones. Developing that ability to listen better has helped my life dramatically. And I'm grateful to all the animals that have been such wonderful teachers. I'm sharing my stories and experiences in the hopes that it helps others open up to listening to their innate abilities and honing their skills. It is such a deeply moving and intimate experience to have with another being to perform energy work with them.

# The Science Of Energy Work:
## Not Just a Bunch of Woo

Anyone that has felt a forehead to see if there is a fever has experienced Energy Work. The body is fighting an infection of some sort and heat is generated in that spot as the increased energy of the body is battling off the foreign invaders. Each organ (skin being an organ), has mass to it and so it fits with Einstein's equation $E=mc^2$. (E is the symbol for energy, m is mass, and c is the speed of light). In other words, if there is a change in mass, energy happens. The c represents the speed of light (approximately 180,000 mph) and it is a constant value. Another equation describing Energy is $e=hf$. The h is the symbol for Planks constant ($6.626075 \times 10^{-34}$) and f is the symbol for frequency.

I hope I haven't imploded your brain with physics and mathematical formulas and don't worry, this book doesn't require you to have any science or mathematical background. I am describing my energy work in mathematical and scientific terms to show that energy work is more than a bunch of woo-woo stuff. It really makes quite good sense from a scientific and mathematical perspective that energy work is real. Some sort of energy is generated when something happens to the mass of an object. Water molecules change when heated or frozen. Energy is created or heat is put out when water molecules are moved more quickly as in for example, boiling water. Our bodies heat up as we exercise and burn off mass when we do so. We use terms like calories to describe that action. Each organ has mass and thus has a frequency associated to it.

I can combine those two equations from above and it becomes $hf=mc^2$. In other words, frequency equals mass times the square of the speed of light divided by Plank's constant. Or to simplify further, frequency is related to mass. So when our body isn't working right, the organ affected will vibrate at a different frequency than when it is healthy. Each organ in our body has its own weight or mass and as such, it has its own normal frequency rate. When that organ suffers an injury or illness, it will vibrate at a different rate putting out a different frequency; and, those of us attuned to feeling frequencies can feel the difference and sense where the energy needs to be focused to put the wounded or ill organ back to operating at its healthy frequency again.

When I do energy work, I often can feel a temperature change in an area or some vibrational abnormality that is being emitted by the body. Is there intuition happening too? You bet! I sometimes feel it in my hands where the temperature difference in the body is occurring. I also am experiencing the vibrational change using other senses that go beyond the normal five senses. Many may think humans are limited to only those five senses, but I believe we have way more than that. Our human language limits our ability to describe some of these senses. But just because we may not have words to define the experience, it doesn't mean the experience isn't real.

I also believe anyone can do energy work. But like any skill, some are more talented at it than others and some have worked harder at developing the skill too. Some people are born with beautiful singing voices. They take classes, train, and become world famous opera singers and entertainers, while there are many others that should keep their singing to the privacy of their showers! Some people are totally tone deaf, but can they sing? Of course. So yes, anyone can do energy work if they are open and willing to hone their innate abilities.

I come from a pretty left brain world. I earned my degree in Engineering and worked for the Navy for nearly 20 years. The one person I had to convince more than anyone that this was real was myself. It's rather ironic that my math and engineering background helped prove to myself that it was indeed real. It was my "Ah-ha" moment when I remembered those equations and the pieces fit so perfectly. That was a big shift in my thinking and willingness to really open up myself to practice and learn more about this gift and skill I have.

In this book, I am sharing some of the stories and experiences I have had with my animal friends and the energy we have shared together. And I promise, no more math and physics equations! ❖

# Reiki

Reiki (pronounced Ray- key) is a Japanese energy technique that aids in stress reduction and relaxation as well as promotes healing. I learned about Reiki after my collie took ill. My puppy, Fawkes, suddenly began throwing up one evening. I didn't know if she had gotten into something or if she had fallen ill. I rushed her to the vet the next day and he gave her some medicine, but she was still sick to her stomach. I called my chiropractor who also treats animals. She had me bring Fawkes in right away. I arrived at Dr. Patty's of-

*My sweet collie, Fawkes*

fice and she asked me to wait a few minutes in the waiting room until she was ready for us. Another woman that has an office in the same building and performs massages down the hall was waiting for a client to arrive. She came over to visit with Fawkes in the waiting room. Dr. Patty asked the masseuse, Shannon, if she'd check out Fawkes and see if she "picked anything up." I wasn't sure what Dr. Patty meant since I knew Shannon was a masseuse and not a doctor or chiropractor. I wondered if Shannon did some sort of animal communication. She agreed and bent down to be at Fawkes' level. My collie was very shy especially of strangers, but she walked over to Shannon and sniffed her hands. Shannon did not try to pet Fawkes, but just held her hands out with palms facing Fawkes' nose so she could easily sniff them. Fawkes sniffed and then backed away, but came back and sniffed again. I sat on the waiting room couch observing and feeling that something was going on between Fawkes and Shannon, but not sure what. After Fawkes sniffed Shannon's hands a few times, she gave Shannon a gentle kiss on her face as if to thank her. Fawkes wasn't much of a kisser so the behavior that went on between Shannon and Fawkes was different than the norm.

Dr. Patty came out of her office shortly after I had watched the interaction between Fawkes and Shannon. She and Shannon spoke about Fawkes condition. Shannon said that she wasn't sure what was wrong with Fawkes, but she was definitely not feeling right in her tummy area. She turned to me and told me if I wanted her to work on Fawkes more, to let her know. I thanked her, not sure what that meant or what had just happened in the waiting room, but grateful for the care she had given my little Fawkes.

Fawkes perked up a bit after Dr. Patty's treatment but later that night, she took ill again and started vomiting in the middle of the night. I sat on the floor with Fawkes trying to comfort her. I was worried about her and felt so helpless, but then I remembered what Shannon had done that afternoon. I suspected it was some sort of energy healing. I had never done that myself and didn't know how to, but decided I would try. I figured it couldn't hurt and it might help. At least it made me feel like I was doing something to help my little girl.

Wiley, my Australian Shepherd, was asleep up in the pillows at the head of the bed. I sat on the floor at the foot of the bed next to Fawkes who was laying there with her legs pulled up indicating her tummy hurt. I held my hands over Fawkes like I had seen Shannon do it and visualized pulling away the cruddy stuff out of my little girl that was making her sick and replacing it with nice light oxygen. I thought it made sense to sweep my hands a few inches over Fawkes' body as if I were sweeping away the bad energy making her so sick. I wasn't sure why I was doing that, but it felt like the right thing to do. Wiley, who was sleeping, shot up and jumped to the foot of the bed. He placed his paw firmly on my shoulder and looked at me with such intensity. I stopped what I was doing and patted his paw and told him it was ok. I was only trying to help Fawkes. He relaxed, but kept his paw lightly on my shoulder and laid down to watch. I experienced a chill that made the hair on the back of my neck stand up. I knew Wiley had sensed the energy that I was sending to Fawkes. I wasn't sure I was really doing anything, but by Wiley's reaction, I was certain something truly occurred. I went back to what I was doing and continued to concentrate on sending the bad energy away and replacing it with gentle healing energy. I did that for about 15 or 20 minutes when Fawkes let out a heavy sigh and stretched. Her legs relaxed and she fell sound asleep. I could tell her tummy must have eased because her back legs were no longer tight. I continued for a few more minutes sending her nice gentle energy. It seemed Fawkes was finally going to get some good rest. I decided to get some sleep too. Wiley and I went back up to the pillows and we all slept.

We made it through the rest of the night without anymore vomiting and Fawkes started to recuperate. I had another appointment the next day with Dr. Patty and Fawkes. I couldn't wait to tell her what happened that night. Shannon was there when I arrived and I told her what had happened. I admitted that I didn't know what the heck she had done, but it worked when I did it too. She told me it was called Reiki which is a form of energy healing and the "laying on hands." It is a technique that aids in stress reduction and relaxation as well as promote healing. Shannon told me that she would be teaching a beginning class in Reiki that weekend. Would I like to attend? I said, "Sign me up!"

After attending that weekend-long workshop, I became certified as a Level II Reiki practitioner. The course was geared for humans which I didn't particularly want to work. I mostly wanted the knowledge to help my animals. I hadn't yet gotten involved with alpacas, but after Fawkes had been so sick, I knew this was something that would come in handy with my dogs.

There were only two of us students becoming certified that weekend so we were able to experience a lot during the intensive training session. We practiced the techniques on each other and then talked about what we felt. We opened up and honed our intuitive skills.

As I practiced the techniques on my classmate, I had an interesting experience. She was laying on the massage table and I had my hands placed on her stomach region. It felt like there was a strong magnet holding my hands in that place. I could feel such strong energy pushing against my hands and I had to push back to hold them there. There were times when I just wanted to move my hands as my arms were starting to get tired but it was like I was glued to that spot. I couldn't move them. My back started to ache as I stood there feeling the strong pulse of energy with my hands. I moved my legs a bit trying to get my back more comfortable but it kept aching more and more and even started to spasm but I couldn't move my hands. I had my eyes clothes and tried breathing deeply. I sensed Shannon, who was sitting in the corner of the room, sending energy too. I remember Shannon telling us a story earlier of her spirit guides coming to assist her at times and for us to be aware of them when doing our Reiki sessions. I reached out my mind to see if there might be a spirit guide around to help me. Just then, I felt a presence behind me. I knew Shannon was still sitting in her chair, so it wasn't her. I felt hands cover mine and took some of the energy that was pushing against me. The load was eased and I was better able to hold the position for a few minutes longer. Then the energy seemed to ease and the magnet that was holding me in place lifted and I could move to the next area. My back stopped hurting as soon as I moved to my classmates next area I was to work on.

We talked about our experiences after the Reiki session was over. My classmate told me she had issues in that region of her body, but she only felt nice energy and warmth when I was working on her even though I felt such discomfort. Shannon said that she felt a presence come into the room when I was working on that painful area. She could see I was struggling and she was sending me Reiki energy as well to help me through it. So whether it was Shannon's energy I felt or a spirit guide, I'm not sure, but it was a wild experience. It was also the beginning of a new aspect to my life. At the time, I had no idea of how important it would become. ❧

# Baby Seal, Ducks, Eagles, Gorillas ... Oh My!

I can't tell you when it all really started: an odd coincidence here and there, knowing the phone would ring, wanting to get somewhere but I would find I'd be driving home

*Rusty was my first teacher in animal communication.*

instead of where I intended to be, then I'd get home just as the phone was ringing and on the other end was a friend in crisis. My thoughts would tell me to slow down so I wouldn't be in an accident, and in minutes a car made too wide of a turn and hit the car in front of me. I had time to stop, resulting with the other car missing me by inches. After a while, the little things and coincidences added up.

I became more open to the possibility of something else happening and just by being open and starting to tune into what was going on around me, more things happened. I'd feel a pain in my body as someone would pass by. Not a pleasant feeling and often scary and then it would suddenly leave once the person left my space. Real or imagined, I'd wonder. I started reading books on the subject and found other authors' experiences similar to my own. Experiences I never shared with anyone else and yet these folks described it all. Some wrote about it being a process of development and I could see how from my own experiences that it did seem to follow a pattern and process. Like a human child, who is born able to immediately stand up and walk, the skill develops in stages. Human babies learn to roll over, then scoot around, and then use objects to lift themselves up and hold onto as they take their first teetering steps, until they finally get the coordination and balance to take those first unassisted steps. It takes almost two years for some to learn those basic skills. So when opening up to intuitive energy work, it also grows in stages and develops over time. Much depends on how much one is open to practicing it.

I did a lot of reading about intuitive abilities of others and energy work. I wasn't ready to talk about my own yet so reading about others' lives and skills was a safe way for me to explore what was going on for me. I found a book on doing mental communication with animals. My dog Rusty and I had had such a close connection that I wanted to learn if it was possible to communicate more with him. I was fascinated by the book and loved the stories the authors shared about their animal communication experiences. The book included methods to try yourself.

I found Rusty responding to me when I mentally communicated with him. It was wonderful to be so close with another being like that. Rusty and I loved to jog and walk along the beach. There was a nice path that we could take for miles if we wanted to. One weekend morning we were taking an extra long jog. It had been the day after a rough storm. The sand had drifted up all the way to the road and there was debris strewn about. The waves were still high and the sea was rough with white caps. We reached a spot that was at the far end just past the parking area and about where the path turns up to go towards town. Most folks turn back before that spot which makes the rest of the jog more private, but that day, there were several people looking at something. As we jogged, there was yellow caution tape circling something and as we arrived where the folks were standing, we saw a baby seal. The poor baby was making a mournful cry. A woman had been there when the marine animal workers were there to put up the caution tape around the baby seal. She repeated what was told to her that the mother seal was out at sea fishing but would pop her head up to check on her baby. The baby was exhausted from being out in the rough seas and mom would be out all day fishing but would come back for her baby later that afternoon.

I felt so badly for the seal pup. I could feel how scared it was and tired. I tuned mentally into Rusty who had been the only animal I had tried communicating with so far and told him I might need his help to explain to the baby what was going on. I sent out my thoughts to the baby and told it what the folks had told us. I told the baby that it was safe and that its momma would be back soon for it and that it could just close its eyes and rest. Rusty stood quietly beside me which was interesting because he often barked at other animals. He stood quietly, staring intently at the baby seal. Before I could finish my thoughts, I watched in astonishment as the baby's eyes got heavy and soon closed. I had just finished saying that it could rest safely and it was sound asleep! I looked down at Rusty and wondered if we did that? I watched the seal pup for a few minutes to see if it would awaken and it didn't. It was time we kept going on our jog. We continued along the path towards town another mile and when we returned back, I checked on the seal pup and it was still sound asleep.

In the moment, I was sure Rusty and I had successfully communicated to the seal pup but like a typical human, I started to question myself. Was it real or a coincidence?

Years later after I took a Reiki class and became certified as a Level II Reiki practitioner, I decided I wanted to do it with animals. I was very excited about learning more about energy work. The next morning after my class, I walked to my mailbox. It was located several houses down where the rest of the block's mailboxes were located. On the grass by the mailboxes were two ducks. I had never seen ducks by the mailboxes before. Nor had I seen any after this experience. I thought maybe I could try my mental communication and Reiki on these ducks! I had some stale rolls that I was going to feed to the birds. I picked up my mail and I mentally reached out to the ducks and told them if they would like to follow me back to my house, I had some bread crumbs to feed them and if they didn't mind, I'd like to try doing some Reiki energy on them. I walked back to my house and these two ducks followed walking a few feet behind me. I felt like a momma duck leading her ducklings down the road. My dogs were by my screen door at the front of the house so I communicated to the ducks to wait out of sight so the dogs wouldn't scare them. I ran inside and got the rolls and came out half expecting the ducks to be gone, but they were exactly where I left them. I gave them the roll crumbs and then reached out with my mind and offered them Reiki. I wasn't sure if they were really accepting the Reiki but I did know they had listened to me about following me and stopping where I suggested they stop. They sure enjoyed the rolls and I stood watching and waiting to see if they'd fly off, but they didn't. Several minutes passed and they were still on my lawn. The dogs were in the house by themselves getting into who knew what kind of mischief. I thanked the ducks for allowing me this experience and said goodbye to them. I went into my house quite excited by my experience.

After that, I knew I had to try to do this more. My heart felt so full and it was such a thrill to see animals that I had never met before actually communicate with me or at least listen to what I was communicating to them.

I decided to head to the zoo that day because I wanted to see if my mental communication would work again with other animals. I went to a nearby zoo. Although I don't do energy on animals without owner's permission, this time, I wanted to see if I could connect mentally with different animals. I was not going to do energy to heal, but offer gentle, quiet energy that was relaxing. I was looking for validation that this new found skill was real. I didn't have faith or confidence yet that it was and perhaps more experiences with animals would help me build that confidence.

I first met the lemurs. They were just getting their breakfast. I mentally asked if it was ok to offer them Reiki energy. One of the lemurs eating some fruit meandered over near where I was standing and stared at me. I did some quiet energy on it but I wasn't sure it was just enjoying its breakfast and watching me or if it was receiving any of the energy. I tried a different section of lemurs and another one came down very similar to the other one. Still, I wasn't sure.

I went over to the gibbon's exhibit next. They were on an island. From where I was standing, the gibbons were furthest away from me. I thought I needed to get some sort of validation that they were receiving the energy. There was a giant log on the island that was a considerable distance from them. I asked if they wanted to receive some Reiki, would they please go sit on the log. I knew that if they sat on the log, I would feel confident that they had heard my thoughts and were receiving the Reiki energy since they had to make an effort to come to the log. I waited and nothing happened. I was about to give up when one gibbon came over. It didn't immediately hop onto the log. I was ready to move on when a gibbon finally hopped onto the log. I sent energy to it, but I was questioning myself if it was accepting the energy and heard me or was it a coincidence. Shortly after the gibbon hopped onto the log, one by one, each gibbon came over and hopped onto that log. I felt a chill run down my spine. It wasn't out of fear but excitement. Could this be happening and me really doing this mental communication with animals? A real paradox of my old thinking and new thinking was occurring.

## Baby Seal, Ducks, Eagles, Gorillas ... Oh My!

I moved to the bald eagle exhibit next. I was starting to get a little tired but I felt drawn to the eagle. I mentally asked if it was okay to do energy on him and that I was trying to learn how to do my energy and mental communication techniques. I heard in my head a scolding voice. It wasn't really a voice I heard per se. It felt more like a thought was placed into my head and it felt scolding. It is difficult to explain in words because the human language is so limiting where intuitive language is concerned. The words placed in my head told me that it was a bunch of nonsense and that I already knew how to do all this mental and intuitive communication. I wasn't quite sure how to respond since I never heard in my head a response from an animal before especially one that was scolding me! I replied that I thought he was right but I still needed some validation and if he didn't mind when I was done with the Reiki if he would please raise his wings. Then I'd know I was really doing it. My head was quiet and I didn't hear "no" so I went ahead and offered the eagle some energy. I noticed this time that my left shoulder was aching, almost like an arthritic or bursitis pain. I thought it was because I was holding my arms up a bit. I was trying not to be noticed by the public doing weird things, but I did have my arms up slightly near the fence trying to direct and send the energy through my hands. It helped me visualize the energy flowing to the animals. I thought the ache was mine so ignored the feeling of discomfort. When I was done, I waited to see if the eagle would validate it had received the energy by raising its wings. The eagle raised only one wing and looked straight at me and gave out the loudest caw I had ever heard. It cawed at me twice. I looked down and there was a write-up on this eagle. It had been injured before it arrived at the zoo and as a result, it had one wing amputated. It was the left wing that was gone and after I read it and was done with the energy work, my shoulder stopped aching. The "I believe" button was pushed. With a few tears in my eyes, I thanked the eagle and wished him well. He had been an amazing teacher.

I was pretty tired and I was getting a bad headache. I started to head back to my car. My mind was racing from all my experiences and I wanted to get home to sort through my day's adventures. As I walked down the path, I passed one of my favorite areas with the gorillas. They are such neat creatures. I stopped and wondered if I'd be able to communicate at all with them. There was one gorilla outside in the viewing area. I offered her some energy. She ran to the back of her enclosure. I thought she wasn't interested, but she came back with a big armful of hay. She spread it on the grass and laid down on it not far from where I was standing as if to say, "I'm ready for my Reiki!" There were two areas to observe the gorillas for that exhibit. One area was inside and had a big thick glass to look at the gorillas and they can walk right up to the glass to look back at us humans. There were a number of people there and I didn't want to be near other humans. The other area to look at the gorillas was outside. It was made to look like an observation hut as if we were scientists observing the gorillas in the wild.

For the time being, I was the only one at this location so I chose to stand there to reach out mentally to the gorilla laying down before me. There were signs around the area saying not to make loud noises and by being quiet, visitors would have a better chance to experience observing the gorillas. They don't like loud noises, the sign said. Of course the people inside either didn't read the sign or were being jerks. They were making stupid monkey noises and being loud and obnoxious. I was very embarrassed to be a human and told the gorilla that. I was having a hard time concentrating to send energy to the gorilla. After one loud outburst by some guy in the other observation area, I had a brief thought. Wouldn't it be nice to scare the beejeebers out of those folks? At least, I *thought* I was saying it to myself. Just as I thought it, the gorilla sprang up from where she was laying down and charged the window! The people shrieked, but of course the glass was there and she stopped before she got that close to the glass. She came right back and laid down on her straw. I chuckled to her and myself and reminded myself I had to be careful what I thought!

I tried to clear my mind to send energy to this female gorilla, but soon a couple came and stood next to me. They weren't part of the obnoxious party but they also weren't the brightest humans ever created either. The way the gorilla was laying, it was obvious that she was female. She was laying there so all parts could be seen. But this woman standing next to me kept calling the gorilla a boy. It was "he" this, and "he" that. I was already embarrassed to be a human from the rudeness of the other folks and now I was doubly embarrassed by the stupidity of this other group. I apologized to the gorilla. Just as I was apologizing, this woman said something else really ignorant about this gorilla being a male. As she said it, the gorilla slapped her forehead with the palm of her hand as if in exasperation. I had to leave because I was laughing so hard. It was just a perfect response by this beautiful *female* gorilla.

From my experiences with ducks, lemurs, gibbons, the eagle with one wing and the very humorous gorilla, I was convinced that it was possible to communicate and do energy on animals. It had been one of the best days of my life and it opened an entirely new world to me. There are a few experiences in life where you can say an exact moment altered the path of your life. This was one of them. At the time, I had no idea where it would lead, but it definitely changed my life and opened a brand new door of possibilities for me. ▓

# Alpacas Don't Do That:
# Dulcinea

Dulcinea was my first alpaca purchase. The years prior to finding alpacas had been extremely difficult. So many life issues — a career that no longer suited me, an ailing mother who required a lot of time and caregiving until she passed away, and an arson fire that destroyed my home and all my belongings. It was the perfect storm that led me to make

*My first alpaca, Dulcinea*

drastic changes in my life. How many times do we wish we could have a life to do over? After the fire destroyed my home, I was given that chance and opportunity. It was not an easy thing to get through, but I like to describe and compare that experience as if my life had been detailed on a big white board and then someone erased it all in a heartbeat. But then I was handed a marker and told, "Now you get to write up there what you want." I could leave off aspects of my life that no longer worked. I could make a list of what I really wanted, but hadn't had time for previously or even believed possible. It was the opportunity for a real do over.

The fire also cured me of materialism. When everything was there one second and then suddenly gone, my attachment to all those belongings and things ended. I could feel the detachment to materialism almost immediately. Perhaps it was my coping mechanism to deal with the devastation of all that loss. I decided I didn't want to fix that feeling. It was very liberating to be free of caring about things and working so hard to have stuff and then maintain them. I didn't need things to make me happy. It was also the only positive feeling I could muster. To make sense of it all and come out the other side of this tragedy, I had to turn it into a positive experience. The fire had been started by an arsonist who was never caught. It was important to me for a sense of justice that I turn this horrible nightmare into something positive. The best and only start for achieving that goal was feeling a sense of freedom from belongings.

It took a year after my mother's passing, the house fire six weeks later, and then resigning from my job of nearly twenty years that I felt ready to find a new direction for myself.

I took my first real vacation since Mom's passing after having the house rebuilt and then sold. I drove up to Oregon from Southern California. It was the best vacation ever because I could stop when I wanted to stop, turn when I wanted to turn, go when I wanted to go. I had no real agenda. I just wanted to rest and check out areas where I might eventually like to move. But I knew I didn't have to make any major decisions. I could just try things on for size. I had no idea what I really wanted which made it perfect to just explore and see if something intrigued me.

Each night in my hotel room, I took out my laptop, investigated the area where I was and places I may head to the following day. I drove up the highway and wound up in Bend, Oregon on my second day. I liked it there and stayed two days longer exploring various areas. There were pretty views of the Sisters Mountain Ranges. The scenery changed from desert landscape to trees, and forested land to other areas of pastures and fields. I started to see myself finding an acre or two of land with a house. The idea of getting a bit of land was so intriguing and sounded doable. I wanted a simpler life and that was all I knew at the moment. The trip was the catalyst of envisioning possibilities for my future. It was a future I had never dreamed of having until now. Before, I assumed I would finish my career with the government, collect my pension and retirement, then travel or do what other traditional things one does during retirement. I didn't even realize that I may want some land. But now it sounded like a slice of heaven.

I searched on the internet for ideas of what I could do with my acre or two. I had my two shepherding dogs and thought sheep might be fun. I looked up sheep on the internet since I had never done 4-H or anything like it. The only pets I had owned were dogs. How to care for livestock sounded intimidating. I looked at the possibility of goats too.

They seemed more entertaining then sheep. During one of my internet searches, I clicked on a link to mini donkeys. What adorable creatures. I could barely stand it. I fell in love fast with those cute little tykes. I researched more on minis of different species. The idea of getting a couple of mini donkeys, or mini horses, or even mini llamas sounded so fun. Maybe their small stature made it feel more doable to me than full-sized livestock. I spent hours at night alone in my hotel rooms, checking out all the different minis out there. The white board of my life was starting to get a few more items added to it.

After two weeks on the road, I was ready to be home with my dogs. I missed them and my sore back needed to get out of my car. I needed a good adjusting from my chiropractor and made an appointment within a few days of arriving home. I told my chiropractor about my vacation and finding the mini animals and shared my new dream of having a couple of acres to raise them. She suggested I go online and look up a place in a rural community near where I lived that had llamas. They'd be able to give me information I sought. Being so shy, I was reluctant to contact a stranger, but that night I went online and Googled llama farms near me. Sure enough a farm website popped right up. I read all the pages on the website and did more internet searches on alpacas. It was not a llama farm but an alpaca farm. I wasn't sure what the difference was but I decided to email and ask if I could have a tour. I drafted the email but suddenly when it came time to hit "Send," I couldn't do it. I saved the drafted email and decided to think about it. The next day, I looked at the website again and talked myself into sending the email. But again, when I went to click on "Send," my heart started to race and I felt queasy. I thought to myself how silly my reaction was. It wasn't like I was doing anything other than wanting a tour. They might not even reply back, so what was the big deal? I finally mustered up the nerve to click "send" and did it quickly before I had time to let my fear take hold again. It wasn't until I moved to Oregon and onto my farm that I fully realized why my body reacted the way it did. At an unconscious but intuitive level, I knew that by sending that email, I was altering my life forever.

I started to step away from my computer to do something, but before I took a few steps from my desk, there was a ping telling me I received an email. It was from the farm! It was a matter of minutes since I clicked send. The email said, "Sure! Come for a visit. How about Friday?" I replied back that Friday would be fine. I was blown away at how fast and inviting the email was.

That Friday was one of the worst hot, dry Santa Ana winds I had seen in years. I detest Santa Ana winds. They make my head feel like it is going to explode plus they make me so antsy. But, the owner of Windy Hill farm was so kind about getting back to me so quickly and since I made the appointment, I felt it would have been rude to cancel just because of wind. The wind was blowing terribly at my house, but it was ten times worse there at the farm. The dust and sand was hitting me like a sandblaster. It was horrible.

The owner of the farm and I met and talked in the converted garage/office. It was a huge farm with more than 200 alpacas at the time. We sat and chatted for more than an hour about the business. The owner, Lucinda was prepared with lots of literature and gave me a detailed description of alpacas and the alpaca industry. Women are a big percentage of alpaca farmers. The alpaca is smaller in stature making them easier than larger livestock for some of us shorter stature females to handle. I loved how soft and luxurious the alpaca fiber is. My mom taught me to knit and even though I'm not an expert knitter, I certainly could appreciate the quality of the alpaca yarn I was shown.

I was amazed that less than half an hour from my suburban home was an alpaca farm! I never imagined. I knew there were orchards but never thought about any other kind of animal farms around. My eyes were opening to all sorts of things around me that I hadn't noticed before. That concept was becoming a regular theme in my life.

At the farm, the one thing that hooked me more than anything was how they taught how to handle and do all the things needed in caring for the alpacas. I was in need of an adult 4-H training before I even considered taking on any kind of livestock and this was it! I could board alpacas there and learn the ropes. I could take my time to find my property, but I could learn in the meantime. I wouldn't have to wait forever to get some aspects of my new life started. Starting a new life is kind of like putting a 1000 piece puzzle together without the picture of the puzzle to aid in putting it together. My early visits to the alpaca farm helped to put one of the puzzle pieces into place. I felt that familiar chill down my spine that wasn't fear-driven, but was generated from the idea that something big was about to come into my life. Just like my experience with the seal pup and the eagle, a new path was uncovered. I didn't realize then how altering it would be.

We braved the wind. The ranch owner and I walked around some of the pasture areas for me to meet the alpacas. I had no idea what made an alpaca better than the next. We came to where a cream colored alpaca named Dulcinea was with her little baby girl, named Twister. They were in the breeding area. Dulcie was getting bred for her next baby already. I found out that they breed only three weeks after giving birth since they have such a long gestation period. It is almost 11 1/2 months long so their instinct and most fertile time to get pregnant is about three weeks after birth. I was trying to absorb all this new information. I came home and sat at my computer for days reading everything I could find on alpacas.

Two weeks after I met Dulcie and Twister, there was an alpaca show in the Los Angeles area. I decided I'd go check it out. I knew doing something like dog shows was not for me and I wasn't sure if this was like that or not. I have nothing against dog shows at all. I like watching them but knew they just weren't my cup of tea and if the alpaca shows were anything like that, I may change my mind about wanting alpacas and getting into that sort of business. I never had been much interested in livestock shows at fairs when I was a kid which left me doubting that I'd be interested in it as an adult.

I walked onto the grounds of the show and there were pen after pen of alpacas. I walked around checking it out and also noting how it felt for me to be there. I found the ring where the judging was taking place and watched for a bit. I noticed it was mostly women showing the animals. That was interesting. I also noted that they were all wearing black slacks or black jeans and white shirts. Many were wearing sneakers or boots, but definitely no heels and no one was wearing a dress. It was not looking like a dog show ring so far where they groom and style their animals and wear dresses and suits. I stood there as a woman walked her alpaca past me heading towards the show ring. She was wearing a number and it was obvious they were heading to the ring for their turn to be judged. There were pieces of hay sticking out of the alpaca's hair. Some on its head and some on its body. I smiled at that and said, yep, this is way more up my line. It was relaxed and people were casual. That is definitely my style. I found a seat by the judging ring and watched, trying to figure out what was going on.

I found the booth and pens belonging to Lucinda. I had made my decision. I was going to buy an alpaca. I could have looked around and talked to more folks, but I decided I liked Dulcie. Lucinda offered me a seat in her booth and I told her I thought I would like to come to her farm and buy Dulcie and her baby, Twister. She said, I didn't need to wait to come to her farm and that I could do it then. I replied that I would have to do some financial business first to move monies around so I wouldn't be able to do it that day. She looked at me and said, my handshake would do. I smiled at the thought of doing something huge like this with a handshake. We barely met and she was trusting me to buy these animals on a handshake. Wow! I shook her hand and my alpaca life began. I had to sit down for about a half hour because I was in such a state of shock.

I started coming out to the farm several times a week. I asked if any clicker training had been done with alpacas and if there was any literature on it. There were one or two things online about it, but nothing to show how to clicker train alpacas. I had trained my dogs with clicker training and I was convinced it would work. Clicker training is all about utilizing positive reinforcement techniques to create or modify behaviors. It is the animal training method used by many zoos and aquamarine parks.

The first time after buying alpacas, I came out to the farm, I brought my clicker and some training props to use. I had attended a clicker training workshop with miniature horses and the instructor used a tennis ball stuck on the end of about 2 feet of PVC pipe which was used to lure the horse to where the instructor wanted it to go. The horse would know to touch the tennis ball with its nose and would receive a click for doing what it was asked and then be given a treat. I thought this method might work with alpacas too. My first time trying it with Dulcie was a total failure. Dulcie was having no part of it. She wouldn't come near me to take treats from me. I went home and had to ponder how to start with her. I also questioned myself a bit if I was nuts for getting into alpacas but my doubts didn't last long. I considered it a challenge to get this alpaca to learn using clicker training and it gave me something positive to do.

The first step was to earn Dulcie's trust to take food from my hand. I put the props away and went out to her pen the next time with just a bucket of grain. I sat in the dirt and put the bucket near me. She still wouldn't come near me. I moved the bucket further away. Finally, I found a spot that she felt safe enough to come and investigate the bucket of grain. I clicked her when she put her head in to eat some grain. I moved to get closer and she bolted to the other side of the pen. We did this for many sessions on my farm visits. Slowly she came around. I worked for three weeks to gain her trust. Finally, my patience paid off and she began taking food from my hand. After that, she was mine. Dulcie proved to be exceptionally smart. I was blown away at how fast she learned new behaviors. It took me less than five minutes to teach her to put her nose through her halter. I was expecting it to take weeks, like her taking food from my hand, but it was literally a matter of minutes. I taught her to give me kisses for treats. That was my reward!

*Alpacas Don't Do That*

Lucinda would come out periodically and see me working with Dulcie and I'd see Lucinda shake her head. She hadn't seen an alpaca stick their nose in a halter without being held and made to wear it, or give kisses on command until Dulcie. And when I would arrive at the farm, Dulcie would see me walking up the path and run to greet me. Lucinda would again shake her head in disbelief. Alpacas run away from you not to you. "Alpacas don't do that," she would repeat. It became the standard mantra as the behavior of more alpacas followed Dulcie's behavior.

After my success clicker training Dulcie, I asked if I could try my techniques with other alpacas. It was one thing to experiment on my own alpaca, but I needed permission to try on others. And success with one did not mean it would work with others. I needed to work with others to be sure my adapted clicker training methods would produce similar results with other alpacas. I was given the green light to work with other alpacas on the farm. It was a win/win effort. I was able to develop and hone my training techniques and Lucinda received very well trained and socialized alpacas that became more marketable.

I started with a batch of weanlings. They were sad about being separated from their mommas. They liked the pellets and they followed me into a catch pen made using eight-foot panels. Having a smaller area to work in was more effective to train. With traditional clicker training, you should work one on one with an animal, but I found with alpacas, that didn't work. They didn't feel safe with me alone one-on-one. Having a buddy with them, however, made them feel more comfortable and more willing to try doing things. I would have at least two alpacas in the pen with me and sometimes I would have up to a half a dozen 6- or 7-month old alpacas

with me at a time. They learned quickly. Soon we were playing what I called the halter game. I taught them to stick their
noses in the halter like I did with Dulcie. I'd hold up the
halter by the side piece and in the beginning, I'd lure them
in using pellets to encourage them to put their noses through
the halter. It didn't take long and they thought that fun too.
I'd often have two alpacas trying to stick their noses in the
halter at the same time! They were so eager to do their new
trick.

Lucinda came out to where I was working with the weanlings while we were playing the halter game. As fast as I
could click and treat, I was going from one alpaca to the
other to give all a turn of sticking their noses in the halter.
Lucinda stood amazed as she observed me working with the
young alpacas. Later, when Lucinda went to complete those
weanlings' halter training, she told me that batch of alpacas
were the easiest she had ever trained before. They all were
comfortable with the halter so it was no big deal to have it
on all the way and learn how the lead rope worked too. A
few months later, a new buyer was there and interestingly
enough, several of the weanlings I had trained were the ones
sold. They were so social, that the new buyers fell in love
with them. I noted that the clicker trained alpacas not only
responded to me, but with other humans, and they showed
less fear being around people. This was becoming a more
valuable training method.

I was convinced that clicker training was an excellent way
to train alpacas and could be a big part of my new business
venture. I didn't find anyone doing or documenting any kind
of formal clicker training with alpacas. I hadn't seen any
workshops teaching others how to do it either. I was asked

to teach a workshop on clicker training alpacas at Lucinda's farm and I accepted the challenge.

I learned a lot about alpacas and clicker training thanks to Dulcie. She wasn't an easy one to start with, but that worked in my favor. I had to be patient and puzzle out how to convert the traditional way of clicker training to work with a very skittish alpaca. Dulcie is such a smart alpaca and she doesn't always think as the herd does. She is more independent in her thinking. I had to earn her trust.

Almost a year had gone by and I had learned much about working with the alpacas. Dulcie was close to delivering her next baby. I was so excited. I was going out to the farm almost daily to check on Dulcie. Life seemed to be finally headed on a positive course after years of being so incredibly hard. I was so ready for some good stuff to happen in my life. I kept my phone handy waiting for the call that Dulcie was in labor or that she had had her baby.

It was an early Saturday morning and I was just getting dressed when I got the call. I saw from my caller ID that it was the call I was waiting for, but the tone of voice didn't match the excitement I expected to hear. If I had a stopwatch, I could have timed how long it took my brain to translate and assimilate the sad news. The baby was stillborn. Dulcie was ok. So very sorry. I was too shocked to cry. I said I'd be right there.

When I arrived at the farm, the vet was there. She conveyed her condolences. Dulcie had not passed her placenta yet, but not to worry. It wasn't out of the norm. She told me where the baby was if I wanted to see him. She would do a necropsy on him if I wanted. I nodded my head yes. I wanted to get to Dulcie. I stopped and looked at Dulcie's baby boy. He was beautiful. He had cap of light fawn on his head and another patch of light fawn around his middle with white for the rest of his coloring. He would have been so adorable. I touched his fiber lightly and was amazed at its softness. It was too hard to stay with him though. I had to get to Dulcie.

She was cushed in the maternity area. I could tell she was uncomfortable and she hummed quietly. I saw her and the tears started. I wanted to give her Reiki energy but my grief hit like a ton of bricks. I could feel her sadness. She knew her baby died. I could tell. She wasn't looking for him like some mothers do when their babies are taken from them for weighing or other care and then brought back. Dulcie laid there with such a sadness in her eyes. I sat under a shelter about 20 feet from her. I tried to stop crying because I wanted to concentrate on sending Dulcie healing energy. She was the one that lost the baby after all. But I couldn't stop crying. Instead my weeping and grief grew stronger. My own issues of things not working out, happiness was never going to come my way, doom and gloom thoughts all flooded my brain. I cried and cried under the shelter. Dulcie stood up and walked over to me. Then the most amazing thing happened. Dulcie gently placed her forehead on mine and held it there. It was just a brief moment of forehead to forehead. But that brief act was one of the most genuine moments of connection I have ever experienced. She knew my grief was over her baby and was as genuine as her emotions were. She had come over to share her grief with me. I didn't reach out to touch her and didn't move. I let Dulcie do whatever she wanted to do. She backed away from me and went back to laying down where she had been before. That moment helped me not give up on having alpacas. It kept me from losing hope on the possibilities of good things still happening for me. That moment meant the world.

We humans can spend years in a therapy chair because we need so much validation and processing of our emotions and thoughts. We analyze and think so much about experiences and we think we need time to heal all wounds as the saying goes. But I learned in a moment, if something is pure and genuine like it was with Dulcie, the briefest of moments can go a long way in healing a terrific hurt. My heart still ached and I was depressed for weeks even months, but I had retained hope. The act of genuine connection which Dulcie initiated was a huge and memorable gift that would outlast the pain of loss. It was a gift because, "Alpacas don't do that," but Dulcie did, and she did it with me.

# 1000 Hellos: Serena

The screams coming from the barn sounded like an animal was getting skinned alive. I was walking in from the parking lot of the farm where I was boarding my alpacas

*Serena stands tall in her new home in Vermont.*

when I heard the blood curdling screams. I hurried to the barn to see if help was needed. There was Serena, a white suri, standing restrained in the chute screaming like mad. Several people were off to the side standing calmly and the vet was doing her routine ultrasound on Serena to confirm her pregnancy. Lucinda informed me this was typical behavior from Serena who she said was perhaps her most frightened alpaca on the ranch. She had bought her from someone else who must have been making quite a joke naming her Serena as she was definitely not serene.

That was my first introduction to Serena who would eventually become one of my most important teachers. I was new to the alpaca business and was learning how to care for them. I was obtaining my version of an adult 4-H having never owned any kind of livestock before.

I was experimenting with clicker training my alpaca that I had just bought. This training method is based on positive reinforcement techniques. I had used that training method with my dogs and it had been a great training technique. My dogs learned quickly and it increased the bond between us. They were eager and had fun learning. It was not only a positive method for my dogs, but for me as well. Positive begets positive. I had attended a couple of workshops on the subject and was amazed at the different animals that had been successfully trained using this method. I was enthusiastically supported from owners to proceed with my clicker training experimentation.

Not knowing much about alpacas might have seemed a handicap in training these typically skittish animals, but in some ways, it was an advantage. I had no preconceived notions of what would or would not work. Anything was possible as far as I was concerned. After seeing a video of a clicker trained hyena holding its neck up as a vet drew blood from it with no restraint or handling sold me that clicker training would work on any animal. When doubters tell me that clicker training is just a gimmick or an unnecessary step preferring the traditional choke collar method, my response is, "A choke collar doesn't work too well on Shamu. If clicker and positive reinforcement training is good enough for Shamu, I think it's a good method for me to use too."

As I stood in the barn having my eardrums pierced by Serena's shrieks, I was challenged by those in the barn to try and clicker train Serena. If I could get her to respond, I could get most alpacas to train this way.

The challenge was set. It didn't take me much thought to realize that learning how to work with this frightened alpaca would teach me way more than working with the easier, more accepting alpacas. My mind raced with how I should proceed with her. I knew working with Serena in a large pasture was only going to doom me to failure. I requested that Serena and her 5 month old male cria, Arctic Blast, be placed in a smaller pen by the barn for a couple of weeks while I worked with her. Most of those present that day doubted I would succeed, and I had my own doubts too.

Serena stood in her pen petrified any time a human looked at her. Her posture was hunched and tense. She looked like someone who was waiting to be beaten or eaten. Lucinda didn't know how she was treated before she got her. Serena's mother was at the ranch as well. Although she was not an easy animal to handle, she was not as frightened as Serena.

I didn't work with her that first day since Serena was already so upset by her exam. I wanted to give her a day to adjust to her new surroundings and not associate me with what had happened to her in the barn. The next day, I walked into her pen assessing how Serena behaved with me in her enclosure. She placed her cria between us. This struck me as odd and illustrated how incredibly frightened Serena was of humans. Normal behavior has mothers placing their cria away from someone or something they perceive as dangerous. Fortunately, Arctic Blast, didn't share his mother's fear of me and was actually quite curious. He loved pellets and took them readily from my hand. An idea started to percolate. Perhaps I could use Arctic Blast to build a bridge to Serena. If she saw him with me and nothing bad happened, plus observe him receiving treats, she may get the courage to take pellets from me too. During my first sessions with Serena, I spent most of my attention working with Arctic Blast. Mom kept her distance but watched my every move. If I went towards her, she looked ready to scream and run to the opposite corner of the pen. It took several days, but when I sprinkled pellets on the ground far enough away from me, she'd take a little but she was wary of even doing that much. I sat on the ground and that gave her a little more confidence to take the treats. Serena knew I wasn't going to be able to catch her while I was sitting on the ground.

Getting Serena to take pellets from me seemed like an impossible venture. She wouldn't come close. Arctic Blast on the other hand was having a ball with the clicker and treats. I figured out a method to get him used to being touched. Alpacas really don't like being touched especially on their heads. In one session, I got him used to me touching his head and ears. It happened rather by accident. Arctic Blast was reaching under my legs to get some pellets and he was touching his head on my arm. As I sprinkled more pellets on the ground, he touched my arm again and the idea struck me to click him when he touched me. I placed my hand in a position so when Arctic Blast went for the pellets, he had to touch my hand. The first couple of times, he backed away when he touched me but it only took a few times for him to get used to it and he became unconcerned by my touching him. I went through the same process to get him used to me touching the rest of his body. He was focused on his treats and not on my touching his body. Lucinda walked by at one point as I was touching his head and I saw her do a double take. No words were exchanged between us but I saw her shaking her head as I'm sure she was saying to herself, "Alpacas don't let you touch them like that!"

One session after being unsuccessful again in luring Serena near me, I thought maybe she'd let me do some Reiki on her. Although I was trained to use Reiki on humans, I knew I wanted to use it for animals. I had never tried Reiki on an alpaca before, but decided I had nothing to lose.

I sat down in the dirt pen and took some deep breaths. Serena stood as far away from me as she could. I knew I'd never get close enough to lay my hands on her so I visualized the energy techniques and attempted to "send" the energy to her from a distance. With each exhalation, I visualized sending calm, safe energy to Serena. It became a mantra in my mind. I kept my eyes open to watch her behavior. She stood perfectly still and watched me. I wasn't sure anything was happening and then I started to see her move her jaw back and forth. She wasn't really chewing her cud but simply moving her jaw back and forth. Her eyes started to soften. I kept up my mantra. Serena looked like she was finally calming down. It took all I had not to whoop with joy when she cushed, folding her legs under her and laid down as alpacas do. She kept up her jaw movement and started to chew her cud in earnest as she lay there calmly. I stayed in the pen with Serena for close to an hour. My legs were falling asleep and I needed to get moving but I was pleased that she finally got used to me being there and felt safe enough to lay down. I believed the Reiki actually worked.

The next time I went to the farm, I decided to try doing Reiki on Serena again. The only problem was the vet was there doing routine exams. Alpacas and humans were coming and going out of the barn passing by Serena's pen constantly. There was a lot of commotion which put Serena on an even higher alert than normal. I didn't have much hope that the Reiki would work but I thought I'd give it a try. I sat in the same spot I had previously. I had given Arctic Blast some treats and he soon gave up on me and went to the hay bin when he realized no more treats were coming his way. I settled in and took a couple of deep breaths. Serena stood in almost the same spot she did during the previous session. I followed the same pattern and mantra in my head. This time, Serena started moving her jaw back and forth almost immediately. I figured this was a calming gesture on her part. Her eyes softened again and she cushed. I watched her as her eyes went half mast nearly closing. I continued to send her calm, safe energy and was tickled as I watched her head bob as she fought dosing off. Within a few minutes she had fallen sound asleep. I finished my Reiki on her and sat there in the pen watching Serena sleep. I didn't want to disturb her by getting up. Lucinda walked by at one point and saw me sitting in the pen and then looked at Serena sound asleep. She looked at me with a puzzled expression and I simply smiled at her. I sat with Serena for another half hour and decided I needed to get going on some other training I wanted to do with my other animals. I got up quietly and walked slowly to the gate. I had to walk about a foot away from her to get to the gate and thought for sure she'd jump up. She got up the last time I did the Reiki on her when I walked past her but this time, she remained where she was sleeping restfully. Her posture changed and for the first time, she looked as though she deserved her name. She was truly serene-looking laying there. With the stress eased and fear momentarily dissipated, she looked lovely. She remained asleep for the rest of my stay at the ranch. I checked on her several times and she stayed in that spot the entire time very relaxed and sleeping peacefully even with all the chaos going on in the barn only a few feet away from her.

A couple of days before it was time to move Serena with the rest of the herd, she finally decided to trust me to take some treats. It took a lot of patience and trying different methods before she became brave enough to take food from me. There was a trough on one side of the pen and I'd sit by the trough. I knew if I was smaller than Serena, I was less threatening to her. I couldn't catch her if I was sitting down. She got brave enough to eat from the trough but every time I got my hand near her, she'd back away. Arctic Blast came over and happily ate like crazy. It worked best to have him between Serena and me. I tried everything I could think of. I put my hand under the trough so that she got used to my outstretched hand. I finally got the idea that maybe she didn't like my opened hand so I closed my hand and put the pellets in the trough. If she wanted the treats, Serena had to touch my closed hand to get them. The first time she tried, the touch of my hand made her jump back. I tried again and she came back. It took a few tries before she stopped jumping back in total fear. Once she got more confident with this routine, I tried pushing it a bit further and slightly opened my hand but not all the way and not palm up. She got used to that fairly quickly. I tried to go for broke and turned my hand palm up. This time, she took the treats that were near my fingers. She was more skittish, but I did my best not to move other than putting the treats in the trough. My arm was starting to ache badly by that point as it had been in an awkward position for some time, but we were making the best progress that I had so far with her so didn't want to stop. This time, I put some pellets in my hand as well as the trough. I held my breath so I wouldn't move. She took the treats from the trough and my hand. She jumped back as soon as she realized she touched my hand. I held in my desire to cheer but instead put more treats in my hand right away so she didn't have too much time to think about it. There was more food if she wanted it. Come and get it. She came right back. The next time, I only put treats in my hand and she took it with her normal skittishness. I repeated this quite a few times so she'd get used to the smell of my hand and taking treats from it.

I slowly raised my arm above the trough and fed her as close to a position I'd be in as if I was standing. I saw her confidence improving. I ended it on that note as it was the best she had done and I was so pleased. You always want to end a training session on a positive and nothing could be more positive than what she had done that day.

I came out the day before Serena was going to get moved back to her normal pasture so I could try one more training session with her. I sat down and got her to take food from me quickly. I didn't have to go through all the steps of the previous session. This time, my goal was to get her to eat from me while I stood up. It didn't take long and only a few interim steps before Serena took pellets from my hand. I was thrilled with her. I called Lucinda over and she was amazed that I had actually gotten Serena to take food from me. She saw Serena fall asleep with me in the pen and now take food. She was ready to go back to her pasture with the others.

I felt like I had accomplished one of the greatest challenges of my life. When I told other people about it and how excited I was, I could see in their faces that they didn't get why I was so excited. But that day Serena took pellets from my hand, I knew the power of positive training and Reiki. And, I was good at it. I had the patience, the time and the desire to work with these animals. Working as a therapist, it was always an honor and very humbling when clients trusted me with things they never shared with another human being. Having Serena trust me to take food from me was one of those kinds of humbling and honored moments too. It was also much harder as I had to develop new skills to communicate with her. I had to keep trying different methods until I found the right body movement and position that she finally decided was safe. My efforts with Serena was another new door that opened for me.

Two years later, if Serena saw me in the pasture, she'd look at me warily, but never came near me to accept treats. I had gone on to working with my own alpacas and others and hadn't put any thought or real energy in training her after those first couple of weeks. But every time I saw her, I would say, "Hello Serena!"

One of my alpacas had a new baby and was in the same pasture as Serena and her newborn. I spent a lot of time with my new cria and mom. Serena kept to herself when I was in the pasture. She was good at making herself look invisible in the herd. She wouldn't draw attention to herself when humans were around unless she was being caught and then she would scream bloody murder. I often didn't see or notice her when I'd be in the pasture, but if I did, I'd say hello. I didn't need to offer her treats as she rarely came close enough to take them.

One day, I was passing by the pasture and Serena was by the fence. I was offering treats to whomever wanted some. I noticed Serena and said hello and offered a handful of pellets to her not expecting her to accept them. I was shocked when she took the pellets from my hand. I did a double take and questioned whether it was indeed Serena that was taking food from me. Her name tag had fallen off and I thought maybe there was another animal that just looked like her that was taking treats from me. This alpaca was taking food from my hand rather readily so it made me doubt it was indeed Serena. But Serena has a distinct look and indeed it was her. I thought perhaps Serena was open (not pregnant) and her hormones weren't kicking in telling her to avoid everyone at all costs. Sometimes females are extra friendly when they're not pregnant.

The next day I was out again in her pasture, and this time Serena walked up to me and accepted pellets with me standing right by her. I had planned on doing other work that day but decided that if Serena was not pregnant yet and accepting treats like this, it was way more important to take advantage of her being receptive and taking pellets. I practiced coming in and out of her pasture so she would get used to me approaching her. She never ran from me although she startled a couple of times when I pushed going closer to her. But she regrouped and came back for more treats. I lured her to come closer to me and she had to take her treats with me holding my hand against my chest. I wanted her to experience being near me with nothing bad happening. I got so I could tickle her chin while she took grain from me and I even got to give her a kiss a few times. I went to see her several times the next few days and with each passing day, she seemed to be more comfortable with me. When she'd see me coming, she'd greet me at the gate walking some distance in the pasture to do so. She even followed me in the pasture as I walked about.

I later asked about Serena's pregnancy status and was shocked to find out she had been bred and spitting off for several weeks. (Alpacas will spit at the male if they are pregnant and it's an early pregnancy test that breeders do for about a month before confirming a pregnancy with an ultrasound.) My theory that she was open and more receptive was blown apart. I have no idea what clicked in Serena's brain for her to decide that she was ready to engage in a relationship with me after almost two years. The only thing I can think of were the 1000 hellos I said to her the last couple of years. It took a lot of experiences of nothing "bad" happening to overcome her fears. It was her idea to have a connection with me and my treats. Her interest in humans was transferred to others too. I brought in a couple of other folks with me and she took pellets from them too. She was still skittish and if Lucinda caught her, she would scream like mad. But she had come a long way. Although most owners don't have the time to spend modifying the extreme behavior that Serena exhibited, I was pleased to prove if only to myself, that it was possible. She will always have a soft spot in my heart for teaching me so much about patience and the value of saying a 1000 hellos. 🏵

# Ocean Breeze and Pruga

Serena had more offspring at the ranch. She had a female named Nervous Nellie. And yes, she lived up to her name and had the same frightened demeanor as her mother. Nervous Nellie had a daughter named Ocean Breeze that was about the same age as Twister, Dulcinea's girl. Ocean Breeze was put in the same pasture as Twister and they were weaned

*Ocean Breeze breaks the fear cycle and engages with humans and cameras!*

about the same time. I was working a lot with Twister after weaning her from Dulcie since that is the best time to bond with an alpaca. The human gets to become the nurturer, providing pellets and goodies. I have found that the bond with me happens more quickly if I can be with the youngsters for the days following weaning.

I was doing lots of clicker training with a bunch of the weanlings and Ocean Breeze was really enjoying the game with the target stick especially. The target stick serves multiple purposes. It extends the length of my arm and once they have mastered touching the tennis ball, I use it as a lure to help train other behaviors. It is a great tool to teach them how to bow and to touch their feet to name a few.

Ocean Breeze was a quick learner and enjoyed the game more than Twister or any of the others. Lucinda came out to work in the next pasture to where I was training the alpacas. She watched me work with Ocean Breeze using the target stick. Lucinda asked me if I knew who Ocean Breeze was. I shook my head and replied that I didn't know. "She's Serena's granddaughter and Nervous Nellie's baby," I was told. My eyes went wide and I broke into a huge smile. I was pleased that the clicker training was helping to break that fear dynamic of Serena's which was passed onto Nervous Nellie who was passing it onto her offspring. After my training with Ocean Breeze, she was sold to a lovely couple just starting out in the alpaca business. I was pleased when I heard they fell in love with her because of how sweet Ocean Breeze was and this couple loved how she greeted them in the pasture. They said Ocean Breeze followed them all around and they knew they wanted to buy her. Ocean Breeze found a great home and had a baby of her own who is also a sweet little girl.

## Alpacas Don't Do That

The farm had a large crop of weanlings, one of which was Serena's boy, Pruga, that needed halter training before the approaching show season. I offered to help train them to wear and walk properly wearing their halters and lead ropes. There were more than a dozen animals that needed training and a short time to do it before the upcoming alpaca show. We set up a small pen to catch them and they took turns having the halter put on and going for a walk. For many, it was the very first time to experience having the halter on. I have observed several reactions that might happen. Some stand still as if in shock. Some buck and have a major temper tantrum even throwing themselves on the ground. Some stand like a trip-pod with their nose touching the ground. The one reaction that is the hardest to overcome is when the alpaca lays down in a cush. I put the halter on a little white suri boy who stood there in fear. After haltering this boy, I let him stand still to get used to wearing the halter. He stood there stiff legged and I could see in his eyes how petrified he was.

A couple of us were working together halter training this young group of alpacas. I caught Pruga. He was born about ten months after I worked with Serena during my first days and weeks of alpaca ownership. He took after mom's behavior having the similar fright response around humans. I didn't get a chance to work with him in the pasture like I had done with many of the weanlings the year before.

I tried sending calm energy through the lead rope to Pruga. I took several deep breaths sending him calm energy with each breath. The lead rope is a two-way communication device. Not only can they feel the slight tug to make them walk, but the alpaca can feel our tension or relaxation through the line. When I teach how to halter train, I show students how it feels to be led on a halter like an alpaca. They can experience how it feels to have someone tense on the end and what a difference it is compared to someone calm leading them. I continued sending gentle energy through the line and made sure I was calm and quiet on my end of the rope. I could see he was relaxing as I did my deep, calming breaths. I was talking to the others that were training their alpacas as I sent Pruga this quiet and gentle energy. When I looked back at him to see how he was doing, I had to do a double take since it looked like he was falling asleep. His eyes were half closed and his head was bobbing like someone dozing off. I started to laugh and the others looked over. I said, "He's falling asleep!" We laughed and someone piped up saying, "That has to be a first." This young alpaca went from being scared to death to falling asleep on his first halter training session.

Pruga wound up dozing off on our next training session, too. He was scared again after having the halter placed on him so I repeated my energy work. He immediately calmed and started to fall asleep. I was asked to handle him in the show ring at the upcoming show. But I wasn't sure that was a good idea since I wouldn't want him to fall sound asleep while the judge was looking at him!

I did take Pruga into the show ring and thankfully, he stayed awake. I was very proud of him. He was very anxious before we went in. I sent him some calm energy, but didn't want him to be overly relaxed, so just before we went into the ring, I visualized him standing tall, proud, and handsome. That was a mantra I said in my head to him while were in the ring. Pruga stood perfectly still while the judge examined him and while we waited for all the others to be judged. He stood still despite the fact that the other alpacas in the ring were dancing and jumping around. He stood there proud and with his ears up. He was so handsome. We didn't come away with top billing, but if there was a blue ribbon for behavior, he would have won hands down.

Arctic Blast, Ocean Breeze, and Pruga demonstrated that with a little patience and positive reinforcement training, quiet and gentle energy sessions, and respectful handling, the fears of the mother don't have to continue onto the next generation. The fear-based pattern can be broken, resulting in animals that are easier to handle, more enjoyable to be around, and sell more easily. Serena's family convinced me that my clicker training methods, combined with my energy techniques are intrinsically a huge part of my business model and daily farm life. ▓

# Orphan Annie

Orphan Annie was born a few weeks before Thanksgiving. Her mom was an alpaca named Golden Dream. But, a dream she was not. Golden Dream was notorious for luring unsuspecting people to her. She'd come to the fence looking like she wanted attention and give you a kiss. As soon as

*Orphan Annie leads the other weanling alpacas to me.*

you got close, she'd spit right into your face with that nasty smelling green gunk they bring up from their first stomach. It's really awful. Humans didn't like to be around her and neither did the other alpacas. She was as unpleasant with them as humans.

Golden Dream had a normal delivery and she seemed to take care of the baby for the first few days and then Lucinda noticed that the baby was not thriving like she should. She brought Golden Dream and the baby up to a pen near the barn to watch them more closely and gave the baby supplemental feedings. She seemed to perk up, but when she tried to nurse, Golden Dream wouldn't hold still long enough for the baby to receive nourishment. The vet and Lucinda worked with Golden Dream to get her to nurse her baby. In the meantime, they supplemented the cria hoping the mom would stand still to nurse her baby soon. I would see Golden Dream nuzzle her baby and she didn't like humans to come near which showed normal, healthy mom behavior. But, when the baby came over to nurse, Golden Dream would reject the baby. The baby was confused and was becoming despondent with the mixed signals.

I watched the behavior of mom and baby and it reminded me of the Borderline Personality Disorder I studied in psychology. I learned that the injury to the psyche occurs in infancy. The babies basic needs aren't always met and the baby is left in constant anxiety. It's a very traumatic start in life.

Lucinda told me the story of Golden Dream one day when I was at the farm watching her work to get Golden Dream to nurse her baby. She said that Golden Dream came from a ranch in the midwest. When she was born she was very ill and had to be hospitalized. They saved her, but it was during the dead of winter and they were concerned about her going back to her farm in her weakened condition. It was decided that she should stay at the hospital and be bottle fed with humans to care for her. In the spring she was brought back to the farm. However, she wasn't around other alpacas during her critical early growing up period. She was around humans who spoiled her rotten. Once she got back to the farm, the humans treated her like an alpaca and stuck her in the herd. She didn't know how to be a herd animal since no one had taught her. Golden Dream was rejected in a sense by humans, too. She didn't know how to be an alpaca and didn't fit in with the herd. She was a very confused animal. That explained a lot of her behavior.

Seeing the baby get rejected by her mom made me concerned that another animal was being raised to become a "borderline." I could see her will to live diminish with the continuing rejection. The baby fought against her supplemental feedings. She wanted her mom but mom wouldn't feed her. I showed up one day and found the baby looking horrible. The vet was working on her. There was an IV hooked up to the baby. The doctor wasn't quite sure what was wrong yet, but she suspected that she wasn't digesting the supplemental milk. It might be fermenting in her stomach. It was touch and go for about a week, but she improved. They tried bottle feeding the baby, but with mom there, she fought the bottle. She wanted her mom. In the meantime, Golden Dream was becoming more difficult to deal with.

Lucinda made the decision that the best shot for the baby to survive and have a halfway normal life was to separate mom and baby. If mom was gone, perhaps the baby would accept the bottle. Nix was a midget alpaca that was about 3 years old. She'd would never be bred and Lucinda decided that she might make a good foster mom and companion to the baby. They brought Nix into the pen with Golden Dream and the baby for a few days so the baby would get used to Nix and then they moved Golden Dream to another pasture.

The theory worked like a charm. The baby was named Orphan Annie even though her mother didn't die. She was essentially an orphan. Nix seemed to understand her role immediately. Annie followed Nix as she would her own mom. She stood at her hip and took Nix's cue as to what she should do. The only thing Nix couldn't do was nurse her. Folks took turns trying to bottle feed Annie but she still fought it. Annie wound up weaning herself. They gave her the best hay and alfalfa pellets to try and get as much nourishment in Annie as they could. She managed to eat enough to maintain her weight but she wasn't growing much. She was getting stronger though, and she seemed to be beyond the critical stage. She was going to live, but they weren't certain she would become full grown. Time would tell.

Although the humans put in an extraordinary effort to save Annie, she grew to distrust them. She was handled a lot, but she saw it as unpleasantness. I was asked if I could try my positive training with her to see if that view of humans could be changed. I eagerly agreed. She was so darn cute. It was going to be a treat for me to work with her. She liked the alfalfa pellets and it didn't take long at all before she'd come and take them from me. I'd sit in her pen to make myself small and she'd come and eat them from me. I lured her close to me holding the treats near my face and would kiss her nose. She didn't seem to mind and I enjoyed being so close to her. I fell in love with Orphan Annie sitting in the pen socializing with her.

They moved Annie and Nix into a pasture eventually and she seemed to enjoy being around the other young alpacas.

She was growing up to be a healthy normal alpaca, except she was smaller. I'd go out and visit Annie regularly in the big pasture. She knew her name so one of the favorite things I did was stand at the opposite end of the pasture and call out to Annie. As soon as she heard her name, she came running, quite often bringing the others with her. It was the cutest thing to watch. Although she was a little peanut compared to the others, she took care of herself. She would spit at the others if they encroached on her treats. She was quite often the lead of the herd in her pasture. Annie had become one of the best animals to educate the public on alpacas. She guaranteed to warm folks' hearts and have them fall in love with alpacas when she came running to see who had treats. She loved kids especially and would go up to humans big or small while the other alpacas stayed back and were more wary.

Annie grew to normal size and was bought by some lovely folks and now has her own babies. The key to raising a healthy cria even if they have had a bad start in life, even if they need bottle feeding and a lot of human interference to survive, is to keep them with the herd if at all possible or a maternal foster mom. They need to know how to behave as an alpaca and from my observations, some of the critical times for those socialization skills are taught to cria at a very young age. When we interfere and create a "pet" more like a dog out of a cria, we wind up with a very confused alpaca that is not happy as an adult and quite often ostracized by the herd. They seem to get spittier with us humans as they grow into adulthood because of the rejection they feel as they get older. So who wins? No one. I do socialize my babies, but I am always mindful of making sure they learn to be an alpaca FIRST! I want to see appropriate alpaca behavior and maintain healthy boundaries. I want to see them want to get away from me if I handle them too much. There is time for them to learn that humans are ok types and have goodies for them. It is way more important that they learn to mind their mothers and aunties and understand the language of alpaca.

❖

# Niin

It was a Saturday afternoon and I decided to head out to the ranch. The only people at the farm were the vet and the office worker. I sensed something was amiss the moment I walked through the gate. The first pasture as you enter the property is the maternity pasture. I noticed that a lovely rose gray suri alpaca with a striking white face was pacing back and forth along the fence line. I didn't have a good feel watching her. It was obvious she was distressed. Moms behave in that frantic fashion when they can't find their babies. I asked what was up and was told that Niin had a baby the day before, but the baby had not survived. It had died shortly after birth. It is such a sad sight to see an animal in such grief. People who don't believe animals experience emotions haven't seen this sight. Niin was beside herself and absolutely frantic as she paced the fence line.

I decided I would try offering Anais Niin some Reiki. It couldn't hurt and it might provide some level of comfort. A chair was just on the outside of the fence and I debated taking the chair inside the pasture. Instead, I pulled the chair closer to the corner of the fence, but on the opposite side of the fence so Niin would be able to have a boundary between us. I wasn't sure why I wanted to be in that position, but it felt more respectful to the animal and less intrusive to be in the corner. She had lots of room to be far away from me if she wanted. I took a few deep breaths clearing my mind.

I sent a message offering her some energy if she wanted it. Niin came to where I was sitting and looked directly at me.

I didn't hear a voice in my head but it felt like a thought was placed there. It was an urgent plea asking me where her baby was. The thought tugged at my heart and I felt such a wave of fear and panic coming from Niin. I instantly realized Niin didn't know her baby had died. That was why she was pacing. I didn't speak out loud but talked to her in my mind. I told her how sorry I was but her baby went to the light. The doctor had done her best to save her baby but she was gone.

I was again amazed by the reaction and result of my communication with an animal. No matter how many times I have had this sort of experience, I am still moved and honored to witness their reaction. Niin lowered her head almost touching the ground. She raised her head looking directly in my eyes and we held the connection for a brief moment. Niin turned away from me and slowly walked along the fence one last time looking towards the barn out to where I assumed was the last direction she saw her baby. She got to the end of the fence and turned away. She went to the poop pile and went potty. She looked back over her shoulder once more and then walked to the opposite end of the pasture by the feeders where the other expectant alpacas were standing and eating. I watched as she cushed by one of the feeders. I could hear Niin humming but it had shifted from a fearful and anxious hum to what sounded more sad. She didn't resume pacing the fence line again. Niin's anxiety ended and was replaced with grief. She wasn't interested in receiving any energy so I respectfully left her with her herdmates. She was where she needed to be.

The ranch's office worker came out shortly after my interaction with Niin. She was doing a check on the expectant mom's and to see how Niin was doing. She did a double take seeing that Niin had stopped pacing. She knew I was going to do some energy work on Niin and she asked me what I did. I told her what had happened. Her mouth dropped and her eyes grew wide. She told me Niin hadn't stopped pacing that fence line for almost two days straight. They were just getting ready to sedate Niin, but it wasn't necessary because once Niin knew what had happened to her baby, she had calmed and she simply needed time to get through the loss of her baby.

Niin was a good reminder of how mental communication and energy work help alpacas. My first year with alpacas was more focused on clicker training with them, but that would not have helped Niin. She needed comfort of a different kind. It was very touching and moving to be able to help Niin come to terms with what happened to her baby. It was also a reminder that alpacas are very receptive to that kind of communication and energy work. ▨

# Alpaca Therapy Animals

I invited a local live-in Foster Care Facility to bring some of their children to the ranch. Even with more than 200 alpacas, the ranch was peaceful. I suspected the alpacas would provide a respite from the troubled lives these kids faced

*Mystic Fire as a cria. A few months after this photo was taken, she provided a special and unique moment with a foster care child.*

each day. I had a long-range goal to bring in foster care children to visit alpacas on a regular basis. After discussions with the foster care activities director, we decided that a group of about 20 children would come out for a single visit and we would assess how it went before bigger plans and arrangements were made.

Several vans rolled into the parking lot filled with noisy kids and their counselors. The energy coming out of those vans was extremely high. I was instantly nervous how this would work since the alpacas are so easily spooked. I worried that these spirited, high energy kids were going to freak out the alpacas.

Two extra large livestock guardian dogs greeted the kids. Their energy was dampened while petting the dogs. Some kids were more interested in the dogs than the alpacas and that was fine. My nerves settled quickly as I saw the children enjoying themselves. If nothing else, they were having a good time and sometimes the best therapy is being able to forget the mountain of everyday problems.

The normal tour I gave for farm visitors was thrown out the window as these kids were too energetic to stand still and listen to my Alpaca 101 lesson, nor did they care. They needed hands-on experience with the alpacas as soon as possible. I broke them into smaller groups and took a few kids at a time into some of the smaller pens near the barn.

In the group of 20 children, there were two larger teenaged boys between 15 and 17 years old. They were both about the same height of almost 6 feet, but one was as skinny as a pole and the other looked like he could be a linebacker on the high school football team. The skinnier boy seemed to be more the leader and he was trying to act as if being there was nothing special. He made jokes and teased the others around him over their interest in the animals. I noted his behavior in the back of my mind to observe if the animals would help him warm up to being there. The larger boy showed more interest and asked if he could go into the small pen with me to feed pellets to some of the young alpacas that I had put there for the visit. The alpacas were overwhelmed by the commotion. I gave the kids some pointers on how to engage with the alpacas. The smaller kids were less intimidating to the alpacas and they came over for pellets, but they were more afraid of the larger linebacker kid. I suggested he bend down to be more at the alpacas' height. He made himself small and I told him to hold still while holding out his hand to the alpacas. I noticed he intuitively started to quiet his voice and talk softly to the alpacas, encouraging them to come near him. The skinnier kid was trying to distract the bigger boy and teased him about being with the alpacas. The bigger kid was ignoring the skinnier boy. Before, he participated in the teasing and now he was ignoring the behavior. One of the young alpacas got the courage to come near the big kid. It sniffed the extended hand with the pellets and tentatively took a nibble. Recognizing its favorite treat, it came back for more and was less timid. It ate all the pellets and came back looking for more. The larger boy asked for more pellets and I filled up his hand with the treats. The alpaca came back much more eagerly for the treats. The skinnier kid tried to amp up his teasing to get attention, but the bigger boy continued to ignore him and eventually told him to go away. It was interesting to watch this large boy who had earlier followed the lead of the skinnier kid's poor behavior and then gave up that behavior in order to have a positive experience with the alpacas. He had to choose which behavior he wanted to use. The one behavior was negative and he would receive attention, albeit not positive attention, or he could lower his energy, quiet himself and work to gain the trust of the alpaca resulting in a much more positive experience. Once he gained the trust of the alpaca and was rewarded himself by it, the connection and desire for negative attention was removed. It all happened within 15 minutes of arriving on the farm. I was imagining what positive influence the alpacas would have if these kids could come out more regularly. How therapeutic that would be.

There was also a teenaged girl of about 16 that was also in the foster care group. She was louder than all the other kids. All the kids were eager to get attention, but she was so loud and the counselors had to remind this girl to bring her energy down. I could tell they seemed to keep a close eye on her so I assumed she had a short fuse that had to be monitored. I was glad counselors that knew these children and their dynamics were present so I could just share the alpaca and farm experience with them and not have to monitor behavioral issues. It also allowed me to just observe.

From some of my work with other teenagers and my intuition, the young girl put out a vibe that said, "I'm going to hurt you before you hurt me." She was in a happy mood at the moment but observing the counselors watching her more closely than the other children, I believed she had a short temper. However, she loved being with the animals and she was different with them than with the other kids and counselors. She was gentle with the animals and would quiet down when she petted the dogs and fed the alpacas but with the other children and counselors, she was very boisterous. I could feel her energy hit me like a battering ram. She put out a very intense energy. She approached me with excitement and was eager for my attention. The younger children in the group appeared to want to keep their distance from the two teenaged boys and girl. There was a younger boy of about ten. He appeared to play the role of the scapegoat for the group, especially the teenaged boys. The skinny teenager taunted him any time this younger boy said or did anything. My heart went out to him being teased so badly. He didn't engage in the teasing and ignored it for the most part. Again, I noted the behavior. The counselors were not interceding, so I made a special effort to praise this young boy every time I saw him achieve any good behavior from an animal. The animals didn't care that this young boy was different and actually seemed to be drawn to him. It was difficult not to correct behavior I was witnessing but I took the lead of the counselors and I also wanted to see if the animals would have any impact in modifying the rude behavior or help the boy being taunted without my interference. However, if I felt this boy or any animals were going to be harmed, I was prepared to step in. The counselors were there in numbers to maintain control and they knew their charges much better than me and knew when to step into a situation, so I left it to them to correct bad behavior. I felt for this younger boy though. He craved attention too.

The younger boy talked up a storm to me and acted as he knew everything there was about animals. He spoke with a lot of confidence. Much of what he was saying was incorrect about alpacas but, he needed to show himself as the expert so I let him as long as he wasn't endangering himself, the others, or the alpacas. He needed the ego boost and I was happy to oblige in any way I could to help him achieve that.

The two older boys were my biggest concern with the animals. Their energy was so high, especially the skinnier kid who had such a tough wall around him. He didn't show any interest in the animals and my gut told me that the alpacas were taking attention away from him. As the rest of the kids became more interested in the animals, his acting out increased. At first his antics worked in getting others to join in.

I took the kids to another larger pasture to visit with that group of alpacas. I had worked with some of the alpacas, clicker training them and knew that some were very food motivated and more comfortable around visitors. There were a few shy ones in that group, but several would be eager to be around the children. I wanted to set the kids up for success and I was confident that my alpaca buddies would do that.

The teenaged girl was talking loudly and asking lots of questions about the alpacas. She pointed to one alpaca and said she wanted to feed pellets to that one. Of all the alpacas on the entire ranch she could have chosen, this alpaca was the least friendly. I knew this alpaca since she had been in the same pen as Dulcie when I began my clicker training experiment. The most I ever achieved with this alpaca was to have her come a few feet near me if she was curious about what was going on, but she never took pellets from me or even from the ground if I sprinkled them around her. She was too fearful to engage. There were plenty of fearful alpacas but this one was always in spit fights with other alpacas. She didn't get along that well with any of them and she frequently stood off by herself.

I told the teenaged girl that she was welcome to try but told her not to be disappointed if this alpaca didn't take food from her as she was very shy and difficult to handle. As far as I knew, this alpaca had never taken food from anyone. The girl asked if she could borrow my bucket of grain. I handed it to her and encouraged her to give it a try. The only suggestion I gave her was to turn her body slightly sideways and not face the alpaca squarely as that is an aggressive body stance. Body language is important in working with alpacas especially in the beginning. She took my advice and then I was distracted by questions from other kids.

It was probably less than 5 minutes when the teenaged girl came over to me excited. "She took it from me!" I looked at her in astonishment. "You're kidding!" I replied. "No, she took pellets from me." She asked me to watch, and sure enough, this fearful, mistrusting alpaca gingerly took pellets from her. I was thrilled not only for the girl but for the alpaca. I was relieved that I hadn't discouraged the girl since it was such a special moment for her. I learned a lot too. Of all the alpacas on that ranch, that girl picked the alpaca that probably fit her personality most like her own. I knew then the power of alpaca therapy and what potential there was in bringing troubled souls to alpacas. I didn't need to do anything other than provide the animals and a safe setting. The animals and wounded psyches would do the rest.

I saw that often when I used to bring my puppy to therapy sessions with kids. I took my ego and sat on the couch while the kids and my puppy, Wiley, worked to heal these wounded kids. They knew exactly what to do. I just needed to be the observer and then validate what I just witnessed. That's exactly what I did that day when that troubled teenaged girl managed to feed that difficult alpaca. It may not have had any lasting therapeutic effects since that was her only time out to the ranch, but it showed me what potential there was in setting up a program to work with kids some day.

Next, we went to the weanling pasture. These young alpacas were the show animals and were there to be trained and to get ready for show season. The young boy that had been teased so much the entire time at the farm wanted to go in the pasture with this group of alpacas. I let in a handful of kids including this young boy, and I made sure the skinny teenaged boy stayed out for the moment. This allowed the teased boy some quality time without the taunting.

The young boy picked out the alpaca he wanted to work with and feed. I found it very interesting that this boy picked an alpaca that was also quite aloof with the other alpacas and she had an attitude about her. She was difficult to train and not food motivated, so I hadn't been successful trying to clicker train her like the others in that pasture. She was a real spit fire and her name, Mystic Fire, suited her quite well. I had learned from the teenaged girl and her alpaca though so I told this younger boy to go for it. I gave him treats and walked away to let them bond. I also sent out a prayer in the hopes that it would work as well as the teenaged girl and her alpaca.

The older, larger boy asked to come in with me into the pasture. The skinnier kid teased him about enjoying the alpacas, but the bigger boy ignored the teasing and asked politely if he could come with me. Happy to reward the good behavior and show that it was rewarded over the bad behavior, I invited the bigger boy in. The skinnier kid was upping the ante on his teasing but the bigger kid, seemed to let it roll off his back. He bent down low without me saying anything this time and won over a younger alpaca. I noticed how gentle he was with these alpacas and the alpacas were not afraid of him at all. I was wearing a pouch around my waist that held some treats while allowing me to have the use of both my hands. This bigger, macho boy asked if he could wear my treat pouch. I took it off and let him have it which produced an onslaught of teasing from the skinnier kid. This time, the bigger boy responded and told the skinny boy he didn't care what he said. He wanted to wear it. I was witnessing how the alpacas were breaking the peer pressure the skinnier kid had held over this other boy. It was fascinating to watch.

The skinnier kid decided he wanted to join us with the alpacas and came in the pen with us. He fed a couple of alpacas, but I suspected he was there more to figure out how to regain his control, not to engage with the alpacas. One of the alpacas walked passed him and tried to give him a round house kick with its back leg as it walked by. It just missed the skinnier boy and I exclaimed, "Whew! That was close and that kick would have smarted." I was relieved that it was a miss as I didn't want anything bad to happen while these kids were there. It was interesting that it was an alpaca who is usually very friendly that gave a swipe at this kid and he was the only kid that any of the animals tried to kick or spit at. The skinny kid replied was enlightening, "Ah that would have been nothing compared to what I've had done to me." His comment came so suddenly, I think it caught us both off guard at how much it revealed. His wall slipped for just a second and then went right back up. He left the pen and stayed more aloof while the rest of us visited with the animals.

Meanwhile, the younger boy was still working with Mystic Fire. I looked over to see how he was doing. He was sitting in the grass in the corner of the pen with Mystic Fire. The scene before me nearly brought tears to my eyes as I witnessed them with both of their heads hanging low. Their foreheads were touching. They were in their own world, just the two of them. I knew more alpaca magic was happening. It reminded me of when Dulcie did that with me when we were grieving over her baby. There was something not only mystical happening between Mystic Fire and this young boy, but wonderfully magical.

As the kids got back into the vans to head back to the facility, the skinny kid had managed to resume some of his control and he regained center of attention by teasing the younger boy. The younger boy could care less about the teenaged boy. He was talking away about his time with Mystic Fire not caring if anyone was listening. He walked out with me and talked a mile a minute about her. I thought it an interesting metaphor that while I talked to this young boy about Mystic Fire, the skinny kid jumped into the van and locked the door not allowing this young boy back in the van until the counselors stepped in. The doors and walls were back up and locked between him and that which took away his power and influence. He didn't want to be engaged and didn't like that the other kids allowed themselves to let their walls down even if it was for a couple of hours.

Starting an alpaca therapy program is a dream I still have. I know after my day with these foster kids that these alpacas can do amazing work in aiding wounded souls. ❋

# Opus

Opus was one of the first cria born on my new farm in Oregon. He was my first cria's first cria! He was also one of the best born to me that season. I was going to take him to an alpaca show after he was weaned. He had beautiful fawn fleece with nice tight locks and loads of luster. His mom, Serenade had won a first place blue ribbon and his father, Makeanu, is an excellent herdsire. I was very thrilled with him and looked forward to taking him to a spring alpaca show.

I had the vet out to do the exam needed to transport and be accepted into the show. The vet came out to my farm

*Opie sunning himself shortly after birth*

about a week before the show to do the exam and fill out the required paperwork. We were going to head to Southern California to the show and I was planning on see friends for the first time since moving. I was very excited for my trip away from the farm. The exam went well and we had all our papers in order.

A couple of days after the vet was out to my farm, I was working in the house at my computer and could see the alpacas from my window. Something about Opus struck me as not right. I put my boots on and went out to see if he was ok. He was in my big field and normally if I went up to him, he would immediately get up and run away. He was the least social of the babies. He was cute and sweet, but he didn't like being handled that much. I walked up to him slowly and he didn't get up. My concerns grew as I walked right up to him without him moving. I reached down and patted his back while he continued to lay still. That was a very bad sign which meant he could be sick.

I went back to the barn to get a halter and lead rope. I wanted him by the barn to keep a close eye on him and maybe take his temperature. I came back to the big field and he was still in the same spot. I haltered him. He got up and followed me but was stumbling a bit. He seemed weak. We got back to the barn area and I unhooked his lead so he could rest under the tree if he wanted. I stood back to watch what he would do.

I watched for just a few moments and my concern went to full panic as I watched Opus stumbling and walking right into my two very large Douglas fir trees. He couldn't see! I called Ann, my nearest alpaca farm neighbor and friend, and then called the local vet. Both came over as soon as possible. Opus was declining rapidly. I went into the other pasture and caught his mother, Serenade to be a comfort to him. She seemed to know something was wrong. She let out such a whine as I haltered her up as if she were telling me to hurry so she could get to her baby.

I made a smaller catch pen so Opus could be contained. I didn't know if what he had was contagious either so he needed to be isolated. The vet arrived and examined Opus. He wasn't sure what was wrong but took some blood and gave him a shot of Thiamine hoping that might help with the neurological problem Opus was having. As soon as the shot was administered, Opus went into a convulsion. We watched helplessly as Opus struggled. I held him in my arms sending him as much energy as I could. He quieted and laid in my arms. The vet looked concerned and I could tell by his face that he didn't have much hope. He left more medicine and told me I should give it to him in about 12 hours. I had some homeopathy on hand and I started to give him that as we waited for the test results.

I bundled myself up to stay outside with Opus and give him the homeopathy and syringe water into his mouth to keep him hydrated as best I could. He barely moved. Serenade hummed to him. I stayed with Opus almost the entire night. Around 2 in the morning, he had another bad convulsion. I thought he was going to die, but I held him and poured energy into him. Sweat was pouring down my face even though it was nearly 30 degrees outside. I called on the alpaca spirit guides and asked them for help. I could feel a presence with me as I envisioned pouring energy into him. Serenade stood over us humming to Opus and I could feel some of the other alpacas watching. Opus came out of his convulsion and was weak but still alive. I kept up my energy work trying to visualize whatever bad energy was in him to be removed and replaced with sweet, gentle, healing energy.

I was completely exhausted by about 4 am. I was freezing and completely spent. I knew there was nothing more I could do and Opie seemed to be resting as comfortably as could be expected. I was afraid Opus wasn't going to make it. If he was going to suffer as terribly as he had that night, I would make that horrible decision to put him down. I couldn't see him having more convulsions.

I checked on Opus at first light. He was still laying there weak, but amazingly still alive. I was not sure if I needed to make the call to put him down or not. I would confer with the vet after seeing what the test results were. Being blind and having convulsions was not a good prognosis. I spoke to the vet. Opus had some parasite issues but the vet wasn't sure if that was causing the neurological problems. We could send him to Oregon State University Veterinary Hospital, but that would be very costly and I couldn't afford that. We decided to just watch him for a few more hours. The vet had other calls to make but would stop by later in the afternoon and if need be, we would put Opie down. I checked on Opus every half hour. I went out around 9 am and noticed he had moved, but was lying down again. By 10 am, I saw a miracle. Opus was standing and eating in the hay bin with his mom! He was still blind, but he was up and eating! I gave him more homeopathy. The vet came later that afternoon and gave me antibiotics to try and some other medicine to treat the parasites. I continued giving him homeopathy and energy the rest of the day and I watched as he grew stronger and stronger. No more convulsions, but he still had no sight. He was able to find his food and water. Serenade was taking good care of him.

Opie regained a little sight in one eye but was left totally blind in the other. We have no idea what was wrong with him, but he is now a strong and happy boy. The only thing I can think of that saved him was the homeopathy and energy work I did on him. He hadn't been given anything but the Thiamine which appeared to make him have convulsions.

Opus adapted to his limited sight and learned to follow his herdmates. He also knows his name and if he was left in the field when the others in his group had come in, I would go out and call him. He would follow my voice and then follow me back to his sleeping pasture. Opie's show days were over before they began, but at least he lived. Opie was bought by a wonderful new owner and he lives at Peaceful Sanctuary which is a vacation rental property. He and his alpaca buddy have lots of visitors who love to give him carrots and spoil him rotten. Opie has a wonderful role in life giving pleasure to vacationers. ▩

# Napping in the Show Ring

I was asked to help handle a young alpaca in the show ring. This particular event is called "Get of Sire." Three offspring from a single sire are shown before a judge and the ribbon is for the herdsire, not the offspring. That event identifies if the herdsire can throw his good qualities consistently to his offspring. With three alpacas to be shown simultaneously, three handlers are required. Prior to this event, I was on the sideline watching the judging when I was asked if I would help show one of the three alpacas. I was happy to assist.

I had never handled this particular alpaca before and didn't know anything about him or what he was like on the halter. He was very skittish and jumpy as I worked to keep him standing in one spot in the ring. Our group of three were one of the first to be examined by the judge. The boy I was handling held up ok for the examination, but there were a lot of alpacas to be looked at so it was going to be a long wait before the final outcome and ribbons handed out. This little guy was dancing and unable to hold still. I worked to keep him in the right spot, but he was so scared. I reached over and gently held his neck, massaging it and taking slow deep breaths, hoping it would help calm him. He seemed to settle down a little. He found a spot to stand near his sister, and that also appeared to help calm him. Since the judge was examining others, I didn't worry about having him lined up perfectly at that moment. I kept doing my calm breathing techniques and sent energy to him. I did that for about five minutes and could tell he was relaxing. The lead line slackened and I could feel his body grow less tense. I looked down at his eyes and they were softening and not as fearful. I kept sending the energy to him and looked around to observe the other animals. When I looked back at the alpaca I was holding, I was surprised to see that he had put his head on his sister's back and had fallen sound asleep. I nudged his owner to have her look at what her little boy was doing. We both giggled quietly at our sleeping angel. I hadn't meant to have him so relaxed that he would fall asleep, but I had never imagined an alpaca, especially one as frightened as he had been, would ever fall asleep in a setting like that! We didn't win any blue ribbons that day, but I saw again, the power of energy work and how receptive alpacas are to it. ▨

# Receiving Energy

I went to Florida many years ago to attend a Clicker Training workshop. I had some down time after the last day before my flight out the following day. I decided to go to Sea World because I felt in need of an animal fix. The workshop was about how to use the clicker and positive reinforcement techniques to coach children in sports and with special needs children. It was not a workshop for animals.

I had fun walking around the park and even had some interesting mental communication with some of the sea life.

*Cindy giving Jasmine a massage, but also receiving alpaca energy in return*

The sea turtle was a real kick. They were just beautiful with the most interesting markings, especially on their underside. I asked one if it wouldn't mind raising its flipper so I could see its beautiful markings better and every time it swam past me, it would raise its flipper!

I wasn't at the park very long when I started to get a headache. I have since learned that being in large crowds is not good for me. Now I know to bring my energy field in closer to me, but back then I didn't know any better. When people talk about their personal space, that is what I mean by energy field. Most people's energy field or personal space is about the length of their arm. They can be comfortable with people, especially ones they don't know, about an arm's distance away from their body. If someone walks through that space, most people sense the other person being there. It can be quite uncomfortable and I'm sure most people have experienced that feeling of someone getting into their space. For me, my personal space is much further than my arm. If I have my energy wide open, it can be over a block away! I have been told that from other intuitive people. When my intuitive side was first opening up, I could suddenly feel others' illnesses. It was very disconcerting to feel a sudden headache or other pain in my body. Then as they left my space, the pain would leave just as quickly as it came. I spoke to a more experienced intuitive person about these impressions and feelings because it was so uncomfortable and unnerving. They taught me about this personal or energy space we all have and showed me how I can control it. It isn't a fixed amount of space.

I attended a Healing Touch for Animals workshop. One of the first lessons we practiced was feeling each other's energy fields. I was in a chair as one of the other students was trying to feel my energy field. She was out about an arm's length but not feeling the slight pressure or resistance when you touch the other person's field. The instructor was watching us and she came over, bent over to whisper in my ear. She told me to suck it in. I knew immediately what she meant and quickly brought in my field so the student could feel it. I forgot that my field went far out.

But at Sea World, I hadn't learned about my energy field yet. When in large crowds, I have no idea how many people cross through my space and I almost always get a migraine. So my trip to Sea World was one of those times. I was only there a couple of hours when my headache got really bad. Before I left, I wanted to see the dolphin show. I decided to stick it out until the next show and then head back to my hotel and rest. I entered the dolphin show area and sat down in a quiet spot away from most of the crowd. It was a slow day at the park, so fortunately there wasn't a huge crowd. There were a few dolphins swimming around the pool but the show hadn't started yet. They were there for us to watch and enjoy before things started.

I was tired and felt terrible but I reached out to see if I could communicate to the dolphins swimming in the pool. I asked if they could hear me would they swim upside down (bellies facing towards the surface). One complied and turned over as it passed in front of me. It went around the circle of the pool and always turned over as it passed in front of me. As it went by one time, I heard in my head, "We can help with that." It was one of those voices that really isn't a voice but a thought placed in my head. I knew they meant to help with my headache. I wasn't sure how they were going to help, but I said, "Sure!" As soon as I agreed to accept their help, I felt a pulse of energy hit my body. It reminded me of when I saw the Space Shuttle lift off and the vibration I felt before the sound hit me. I felt the shock wave before the sound reached my ears. It was such an intense feeling. Unlike the Space Shuttle, there was no sound that came with the vibration that washed over me from the dolphins. My headache was instantly gone. I was left with how you feel after a migraine. It felt like it still could come back, but at least I didn't have the horrible pounding leaving me almost nauseated which I had felt just a second before. I thanked the dolphins for helping me and sat back to enjoy the fun show.

I decided I would not push my luck after the show and headed to the hotel to rest and have a quiet evening away from people. That was sure an amazing experience receiving energy from an animal. Dolphins are not only gifted teachers of energy, but providers. 🌸

# Hmm...I Didn't Know
# Two-Leggers Could Do That:

## Thoughts from Jamilah

One of the best ways to learn about the handling and care of alpacas' needs is to volunteer during shearing. It is fantastic training along with lots of hard, filthy work. If you aren't experienced at haltering an alpaca, you will be by the end of one day of shearing. Want to learn how to trim toe nails? It

*Nice hair-do, Jamilah!*

is the perfect time to learn to trim nails. Don't know how to draw or give shots, or give an alpaca de-worming medication? You become experienced when you have to give two shots per alpaca and you shear over forty in one day!

When I was learning, I wanted to work at a different station during each day of the week of shearing. That way I could learn so many things required when it was time to start my own ranch. Some jobs are not my favorites though. But perhaps my favorite station back when I was learning and boarding my alpacas was the role of haltering the alpacas and holding them until it was their turn to go in for shearing. I would do energy to calm them and mentally communicate with the alpaca telling them what was about to be done to them. I believe it helps alpacas to be less afraid when I do this, and I have found them to be more cooperative too. I could only imagine how frightening it was to wait outside the barn and hear other alpacas screaming, the loud noise of the shears, plus see all those humans about. They must have wondered if their herdmates were being slaughtered and they were next. The shorn alpacas didn't look the same when they came out of the barn so they weren't recognized as the same animal that went into the barn. Shearing days are very stressful for alpacas.

When I worked the on-deck station, I mentally told the alpaca what was going to happen to them as I haltered and walked the alpaca to the barn to await its turn. I mentally pictured it all. I visualized to them that this day was the one day each year alpacas were asked to do something in return for having all their needs met the rest of the year. Alpacas were going to get their haircut, nails trimmed, given a couple of needle pokes for administering their vaccines and some nasty tasting de-worming goop. But, after all that, they would be taken back to their pasture to go back to their normal grazing. I reminded them, it would feel so much better having all that hair off. I added that it was ok to scream, pee, and spit if they wanted. They would be just fine when it was all done. I focused sending them gentle, calming energy to help settle their jitters. Many of the alpacas who received my "talk" and energy did indeed calm down. They moved closer to me as I pictured the gentle energy flowing through their bodies. Some placed their chin on my shoulder or hid behind my back. I didn't touch them but simply held the lead rope to keep them in our holding area. They had six feet of the lead rope to distance themselves from me, yet almost all stayed close accepting the energy.

By the end of a shearing day, my energy waned. It was exhausting with many miles of walking or standing nearly the entire day with only short breaks. Although performing energy work is often exhilarating, doing anything all day is tiring. After having said the same mental script over and over all day, it had become more a monotone list of activities I repeated to the next alpaca heading into their shearing. By day's end, the energy was still offered and given but not with as much focus as earlier in the day. I had just haltered up a lovely black Suri female for her turn to be sheared. I started my mental telepathy with her. By then, my mental dialogue was so routine. I had barely started my "talk" when this female did the funniest double and then triple take. She put her nose and face right up against mine sniffing my face. In my head, I felt the words placed in my mind that said, "Hmm, I didn't know two-leggers could do that!" She moved away from me by a foot or two and stood calmly as she accepted the energy I offered her.

## Alpacas Don't Do That

I have to say, this alpaca's two-legger comment tickled me. I hadn't thought of us humans in that fashion but it made perfect sense that they would see us that way. What funny creatures we must be to them using only two legs to get around. Since then, I often think of us humans in that fashion. It helps to remind me that we are not so different as we humans think we are from the rest of the animal species. We think we are. but we could learn so much more if we could accept that sometimes animals are wiser than us and can actually teach us a thing or two if we weren't so darn egotistical!

At the time of shearing, I didn't know who this female black alpaca was. There were so many alpacas on the farm and I spent most of my time with the weanlings or my own two alpacas, Dulcie and Twister. After Dulcie's baby died, I knew I wasn't going to be able to wait a year to have another baby. I enjoyed seeing the other babies but I really wanted one of my own. When the opportunity arose to buy a couple of suris, I didn't hesitate. They were both pregnant and due in a few month's time. My wait for my first alpaca baby wouldn't be long.

After I purchased these two suris, I added them to my visits and offered them treats. Jasmine, a beautiful reddish brown suri, was a bit more shy but liked the pellets and tentatively took some from me. Jamilah, a lovely black suri, was more outgoing but she had an attitude. She would spit at either me or the other alpacas around her when I fed her treats. If she was in a mood, watch out.

One day I went out to give Jamilah some treats. She had long straight black bangs that covered her eyes, making it hard to see. She would sometimes shake her head back to make her bangs fall to the side so she could see better or she would just tilt her head back so she could see under her bangs. I was giving her some treats and I unconsciously made the big mistake of mimicking Jamilah by tilting my head back as if to look at her just as she was tilting her head to look at me. I was rewarded with a smattering of spit right in my face. That wasn't pleasant. At first, I was upset with her. I was offering her treats so why did she spit at me? I realized that alpacas use body language a lot to communicate with each other. Their body language of tilting the head back is a warning that says, "I'm about ready to launch some spit." When I tilted my head, Jamilah saw me threatening her over the treats. She spat at me before I could spit at her. I remembered that lesson and was more mindful of not tilting my head back unless I meant it!

Jamilah and Jasmine's babies were due within a couple of days of each other. I went to the farm nearly every day as their due dates approached and gave them goodies each time. They were in the maternity area which had fewer alpacas, resulting in less competition for treats. Jasmine was so uncomfortable and huge with pregnancy. She learned to trust me quickly since I never handled her, but simply gave her goodies. The last week or two before she had her baby, she wouldn't bother to get up and accepted her treats while remaining cushed. It was too much effort to get up and once she found a comfortable spot, she wasn't moving. Jamilah, on the other hand, wasn't that trusting yet and would stand if she was laying down. She wanted to be ready to spit or walk away if she felt threatened. Jamilah was still a bit spitty at times and after her baby was born, if you went near that baby, you were going to get "greened" with spit big time. Both Jamilah and Jasmine rewarded me with two beautiful baby girls within a week of each other. I was so excited and thrilled.

After the babies were born, I wanted to socialize with them. The moms' hormones seemed to level off after about a week. When alpacas aren't pregnant, they are often much sweeter. Jamilah still didn't like it if I touched the babies but she liked her treats. If the baby came and sniffed me, that was ok as long as I didn't touch or try to take her baby to get weighed. She didn't like that at all. I would sit in the pasture and offer the moms treats and hope the babies would come to me and say "hi."

One day, I was sitting under a tree relaxing near Jamilah and Jasmine. Jamilah was standing behind me. I had given out all the treats, so I just sat there communing with them. Jamilah's chin must have had a terrible itch and she decided that my head would make a good scratching post. She started to rub her chin on my head! It startled me at first but also cracked me up that she was doing it except that it rather hurt. I reached up and said, "If you want your chin scratched, I will scratch it with my hand because that hurts my head to use it as your scratching post." I fully expected her to bolt away from me as I reached up but instead, she let me scratch her chin. I thought that was pretty cool. I kept scratching her chin and then she let me rub her neck. I was very pleased to be allowed to rub the neck of an alpaca without her running away. Jamilah allowed me to rub her neck and down her shoulder. Her fiber was so soft. I slowly, and gently rubbed her, fully expecting her to pull away at any time. But instead, I saw her legs buckle a little and she decided to cush right next to me! I kept rubbing her neck and then her back, starting to apply a little more pressure. I rubbed her back like a real massage and she relaxed into it and began chewing her

I Didn't Know Two-leggers Could Do That

cud. Even though I was so excited by what was happening, I could feel myself relaxing like I was the one receiving the massage. The energy she was pumping out was heavenly. I looked around hoping someone would be a witness to this. But there was no one. I had no witness to this amazing event and then I didn't care because it was just too special. I just wanted it to last forever. Talk about alpacas don't do that! I explained what happened when I saw others later, but I could tell they didn't quite believe me or grasp what I was describing. I'm not sure if they didn't grasp it because alpacas aren't known for wanting full body massages or because it was Jamilah who was accepting the massage, an alpaca known for turning you green if you looked at her.

The next time I went to the farm, I hoped it would happen again. I treated Jamilah and Jasmine with their pellet goodies. They both stood there and let me rub their necks and soon they both cushed, one on either side of me. I sat between my two alpacas and gave them full body massages. I was in heaven. I have had my own massages before and they are wonderful, but to give an alpaca a massage is as Zen an experience as receiving a massage yourself. The alpacas pump out such amazing energy when they are in that state. Other alpacas came over and sniffed Jasmine and Jamilah's rear ends and would often cush nearby us chewing their cuds and enjoying the energy even without their own massage.

After I found the property that I was going to purchase, I went to the farm where I boarded my herd. I wanted to mentally picture to my alpacas the farm I had found for us. I went to Jamilah who had recently had my second baby with her. She was interested in a massage. After she cushed, I sat by her side massaging her gently and began telling her about the farm I found for us. She crooked her neck around to look at me and reached back giving me a kiss on my cheek and nuzzled my face. She had never kissed me before. But now, Jamilah kissed me over and over as I told her about our new home. I could feel her joy in my head. Immediately, I "heard" or felt that same experience in my head just like a couple years before when we were shearing when I had heard, "Hmm, I didn't know two-leggers could do that." I realized then that it was Jamilah who had communicated back to me and had acted so surprised that a human could communicate mentally with them.

Jamilah and I have a close bond. She is my forever girl. She is a great dam who makes wonderful babies and she is a character and a half. Jamilah also is very wise. She is the quiet head of the herd. Others sound their trumpet-like alarm and act as guardians warning of potential danger and act as the dominant personalities. But, the herd quietly looks to Jamilah as their leader. If she looks up and senses there is nothing to be worried about when others are alarming, then soon the rest of the herd relaxes. But, if Jamilah is upset, then the rest of the herd knows to stay alert and wary. Jamilah and I also butt heads from time to time. She can royally tick me off with her attitude. I never know when she will spit at me or kiss me. Yet, I so respect her and she has taught me so much about alpacas and dealing with life issues in the alpaca way.

I bred Jamilah to my new National Champion herdsire I purchased after I moved to Oregon. I was very excited to have his first baby with Jamilah, my most trusted and experienced mom which added to my excitement. What a great beginning on my new farm to have this amazing male as my stud to my females. He won so many first place ribbons in shows all over the country. Jamilah's babies have been consistent show winners too. Combining the two gave me such high hopes for a real prize-winning baby.

It was a hot summer and I was being careful to keep my animals cool by regular hosing them down, especially my very pregnant girls. Jamilah wasn't due for another three and a half weeks when I looked out my window and saw her in labor. I rushed out petrified. It was way too early for having a baby. They don't usually survive that early. The baby came quickly and was alive. I had hope. It was a beautiful medium fawn little girl and I was thrilled it was a girl. She was small but active. She was feisty and wanted to stand and do the normal things you want to see. But she was having a hard time standing to nurse, so I moved them to a shelter penned area where I could work with the baby and Jamilah without the other alpacas interfering.

Normally, Jamilah would spit at me terribly if I touched a new baby of hers, but this time, she allowed me to work with her baby trying to get her to stand and place her under Jamilah to see if she would nurse. She was too young to figure it out so I tried bottle feeding her. I was able to milk out Jamilah to get the precious colostrom so necessary for a baby's immune system. But the baby was not taking much from the bottle. When the baby rested, I saw her stop breathing a few times and I would rub the baby vigorously to get her breathing started again. I did my energy work on her to pump as much energy into her survival center and lungs. After a couple of hours of being unsuccessful of getting the baby to nurse and seeing her stop breathing multiple times, I knew I needed to get her to the hospital if we were going to have a chance of saving her. My wonderful friend, Ann, was there with me and I brought my Honda Element into the barn area. I have transported alpacas in this car before.

## Alpacas Don't Do That

My vet called Oregon State University Veterinary Hospital to let them know we were coming with a newborn cria that needed emergency care. I loaded Jamilah in the back of my car and Ann held the baby in the front next to me. The baby was alert and looked interestingly out the window as cars passed us. People would do double takes and smile as they saw this adorable infant sitting in Ann's lap. I turned up the air conditioner to cool off the baby and help blow more air into her struggling lungs.

The hospital was about an hour away. The baby sat calmly in Ann's lap and looked out the window taking in the world around her. Jamilah sat cushed quietly in the back of my car. I was surprised how easily she loaded in the car. She knew we were doing everything we could to help her baby.

We arrived at the hospital and checked the baby in. They placed an oxygen mask over her face. The baby was so cute with the mask over her face. Her entire head fit inside the mask. The oxygen seemed to be helping her. She seemed to crave the air being offered her. She shoved her tiny face well into the mask to get closer to the wonderful oxygen source. Jamilah and the baby were going to need a few days at the hospital. There was nothing more I could do for them. They were in good hands with a very caring staff. It was terribly hard to leave, but I had to get back to the rest of the herd.

I waited anxiously by the phone to hear how the baby was doing but I also didn't want to pester the staff because they were busy working on my baby. It was about 9 pm when the resident doctor called to give me a status of the baby. She was holding her own, but wasn't out of the woods. She hadn't quite figured out how to nurse yet but was getting close. She was getting fluids from an IV and they had given her a plasma transfusion so she was getting stronger. The doctor was cautiously optimistic. I was exhausted from the intensity of the day, so I decided to go to bed. I kept my phone handy in case I received any other calls from the hospital, but I went to bed having real hope we were going to get through this. At one o'clock in the morning, my phone rang. I woke up with a start and was confused. I answered the call. It was the doctor. The baby had just died. She had seemed so strong and was doing better, but just like what I had seen earlier in the day before I rushed her to the hospital, the baby fell asleep and forgot to breath. Her little lungs just weren't developed enough. I was heartbroken.

I wanted to bring Jamilah home. I knew I wouldn't be able to sleep and I needed to be with my girl. She had to be so lost and sad, plus, it had to be frightening for her being away from her herd. I had another alpaca due with a baby any day. Alpacas tend to have their babies early in the day. I didn't want to leave Jamilah alone in the hospital without her baby until the next evening and I couldn't leave my farm early in the day with another baby due any time. I got dressed and drove to the hospital at one in the morning. I cried almost the entire drive. The staff was very caring and kind as I picked up Jamilah. I felt bad for me and even worse for my Jamilah. She knew she had lost her baby. I could tell. She was humming quietly. It was such a sad drive home. When we arrived, I placed Jamilah in the barn area. The others greeted her but quickly left her alone. It was as if they sensed her grief and gave her space. I went back to the house to try and rest myself even though I knew it would be fruitless. I was too lost in my own grief to sleep.

The next few days were such lessons in grief. I was sad and depressed, but Jamilah's grief was intense. I could feel the anguish emanating from her. I made it my job to provide comfort and aide to my sweet girl. I felt pretty helpless for the most part and wasn't quite sure whether it was best for Jamilah to remain in the pasture with the other babies and where she had given birth or be moved to the other pasture. I decided to let her choose. Jamilah would stand at one of the gates and I would open it to allow her to move into the other area whenever she wanted. Sometimes, Jamilah would herd me to the spot where she delivered the baby and she would let out the most sad and plaintive hum. Almost every time I would hear that hum, the Eric Clapton song written after losing his son, Tears in Heaven, played in my head. It broke my heart listening to her hum. She kept nudging me to the various places where her baby had been. It made me think she was wanting me to find her baby for her and bring her back. But of course, I was helpless to do so. All I could do was tell her how sorry I was that I couldn't save her baby. Jamilah knew her baby was gone, but she still wanted to be in the places she had been with her baby. The first couple of days, she paced from one spot to the other. She ate little and let out a constant soft, but high-pitched hum. Such a terribly sad sight. Letting her be where she needed to be was all I could do for her.

By the third and fourth day of her grief, her trips and pacing to those spots lessened and she started to graze. Jamilah still herded me to those same spots and looked at me as if to say, "fix this." I would offer to rub her neck the way she liked, but she pulled away from my touches. I didn't push it and respected her desire not to be touched. She didn't want energy from me either. Every so often, she would ask me to go to the other pasture and I would open the gate. It was interesting that the other alpacas seemed to keep their distance from her. If an alpaca gets moved into a different pasture, they are greeted with the "sniffing of the butts" routine, but the new herdmates did not do that with Jamilah during this grief period. I believe that they knew and felt her sadness and were showing her respect.

Finally on the fifth day, Jamilah asked to go into the pasture away from where her baby had been and that was the last time she wanted to be moved. She stayed in the other pasture away from babies from then on. She grazed quietly and was rather aloof from the others. She was still sad but was getting back into her normal routine of grazing. That afternoon while I was feeding the herd, Jamilah came up to me. She reached her head towards mine and bussed my cheek with a nuzzled kiss. I carefully reached out my hand to rub her neck still expecting her to pull away like she had the last few days, but instead she stood there letting me stroke her long neck. I whispered in her ear how much I loved her and she kissed my cheek again.

While I was focusing on helping Jamilah through her grief, I found myself following her lead in my own grief. There was too much still to be done on the farm to stop. I wanted to do nothing, but animals still needed to be cared for, chores needed to be done. Losing animals is the reality of farm life. It is the lousiest part of farm life. This loss tested me dearly after having a very long and hard year of losses and setbacks. I had placed so much hope for the recovery of my business on Jamilah's baby. Doubts of staying in the alpaca business ran through my mind and I was seriously considering that I had had enough. But watching Jamilah and grieving with her, I found myself getting stronger each day. I still wanted to be an alpaca farmer. I thought if I wasn't doing this, what would I do? The answer was that

I couldn't imagine doing anything else. I had to pull up my big girl panties and get on with life.

Jamilah was the one that taught me how needy we two-leggers are. I once asked her if she could explain the difference in how we grieve compared to alpacas. It was too complicated a question to ask mentally since our human language is so limiting. Or perhaps, my mental communication abilities are too limited. I can only interpret a few impressions placed in my head. But, I asked anyway and the only answer I managed to understand was "It's different." Another word that showed up in my mind was "validation." We humans need so much validation for our feelings. When I was learning to do mental telepathy with the animals and performing Reiki on them at the zoo that first time, I kept needing more validation. I had the experience but that wasn't good enough, I had to have it again and again to believe it. With alpacas, and I believe other animals, they get it the first time. We humans are so needy with our emotions. We can't accept that one genuine act is enough. Alpacas give genuinely and expect you to believe them the first time.

I was having a really terrible day and I went out to see Jamilah. I felt the need to be with my alpaca that can hear thoughts. I didn't want to talk to a two-legger. I walked out to Jamilah and told her I needed a Jamilah moment. I didn't have to explain my feelings of sadness and anxiety. She felt it. Jamilah came right to me and gave me a kiss. She started to walk away, but I wanted another kiss and more affection, but she continued to walk away. I was saddened by it and then I heard in my head, "I gave you what you asked for? Why do you need more?" I understood then how different we two-leggers are to these alpacas and animals and how much wiser they are at handling things. The fact that she heard me mentally and came over to me, then responded to what I needed with a kiss, was genuine and real. Doing it twice or 10 times wasn't necessary. She meant it the first time. I walked away thinking about that experience. It helped me become aware of when an act by an animal or a human is genuine. If you can tell the difference between real acts of genuine kindness and care, then not only is it enough, it is everything, and it only has to be given once to be incredibly powerful and meaningful.

Learning that lesson has been huge. It has helped me appreciate the acts of kindness from friends. Those moments feel like someone wrapping you in a cozy blanket when you are down and troubled. It is true comfort. On the other spectrum, it has shown me that I don't need to keep relationships whose acts are insincere or superficial. It doesn't take much to make a difference with someone. It just has to be genuine. Thank you Jamilah. What a huge life lesson you taught me.

# Welcoming Newcomers

Welcoming new alpacas to the herd that aren't used to the Hum Sweet Hum way of things is always an interesting process. Not long after I moved to Oregon, I had the opportunity to board some alpacas on my farm for some people that were in the process of moving near me. We had both boarded at the same ranch in California and it was exciting that someone I knew was going to be living near me. I still hadn't met too many two-leggers yet. They moved a handful of alpacas to my farm and it was nice getting some income. However, I was a bit anxious about having one of their al-

*New alpacas to our farm, Naomi and Dove*

pacas living here. I had been around her a handful of times in California and she was notorious for being a terrible spitter. Once, she greened me badly, nailing me with a huge wad of green crud right in my face when I was taking her halter off. That sort of experience is not long forgotten. The alpaca named Pistachio, had beautiful fiber but not the personality to match.

I decided to be as welcoming to Pistachio as I could. She had been here only a few days and I was out doing my chores when I had to walk past Pistachio. She was just standing and as I walked by her, I startled her. She jumped and threatened me with some spit, but in that moment, I also saw her eyes and for just a split second, I saw real fear. My heart went out to her and I lowered my head and said sorry for startling her and went on my way. I had thought she was just a cantankerous alpaca, but Pistachio was really afraid. Fear I can work with. Cantankerous alpacas are way more difficult to build trust with, but with fearful alpacas, I can do my energy work on them and handle them with respect and care and often win them over.

Pistachio arrived in early spring and it was still chilly and rainy, but one day we finally got a little warm sunshine. I was filling up a water tub and Pistachio came to where I was standing with the hose. She just stood there and I was pleased that she came near me on her own. I felt she was interested in the water and hose. Some alpacas just love the hose. I gingerly sprayed a little water at her feet and was pleasantly surprised at her accepting the water. I went back to filling up the tub and watched as Pistachio took a step or two closer to me. I sprayed her a bit more on her feet and legs and went back to filling up the tub. She took another step or two closer and raised her leg asking for more water. I smiled and knew I had found my "in" with Pistachio. She likes the hose. I sprayed her some more and repeated the process of filling up the tub and waiting for Pistachio to ask for more hose. The repetitive process established the beginnings of a bond and showed her that I was listening and by repeating the process and having her "ask" for the hose, allowed me to show her that I was listening and giving her what she asked for. If I had just done a continuous hosing down of her, it would have been less effective. She got the same amount of hosing down, but got to experience asking multiple times while I "treated" her with the hose. She hadn't taken food from me and wouldn't for a couple of more months but the hose gave us the same effect as if I were clicking and treating an alpaca with pellets. I was rewarding her with something she really wanted.

Pistachio still spat when I had to halter her and trim her nails but she calmed down much faster and she responded when I would tell her what I was going to do. She stopped spitting as I trimmed her nails and settled down. She learned that nail trimming wasn't so bad and I handled her with utmost care and respect. Telling her what was going to happen made a huge difference. Pistachio began to want to hang out with me when I was doing chores. She would stand near me and I would chat away to her. If someone had been there, they would have wondered who the heck I was talking to, but Pistachio seemed to like the chatter. If I had farm guests, she loved to come stand with us and listen to our conversation. She would stand a couple of feet away and act like she was part of the chat session.

I bought myself a barbeque grill and made the mistake of getting one that needed to be put together. It was raining for days and weeks, but I wanted it put together, so I took it out to the barn area where I could work under a shelter. Pistachio stood near me as I worked. I warned her that sometimes when I put these types of things together, I get to a spot that gives me fits. I've been known to lose my temper and let fly some expletives. I worked for a good couple of hours when I hit that spot when the darn thing was not cooperating. I was tired enough to lose patience and let loose a few four letter words. Pistachio looked at me and walked away. She had been standing there for almost two hours watching me and the second my energy turned negative and unpleasant, she left. As she walked away, I yelled to her, "I warned you!" Then I had to laugh and my bad mood lifted because it really was funny to see her offended by my crankiness.

Pistachio seemed to really enjoy people and started to learn to eat goodies from us. She discovered carrots and would take carrots from my hands. She saw Misty and Dulcie offer kisses to receive carrots and she surprised me when she started to offer kisses to get her carrots. She had turned into this sweet alpaca that was just a lot of fun to be around.

One day her owners came by to see a new baby of theirs that I had helped to birth. I was getting the baby up to nurse while the husband stood by the fence watching. Pistachio came over like she did when guests came to be near the conversation. She stood a couple feet away from him. After we had been talking for 10-15 minutes with Pistachio standing there the entire time soaking in the conversation, he asked me who the alpaca was that was standing next to him. I replied, "That's your girl, Pistachio." He looked at her more closely and shook his head. "Can't be Pistachio." I said, "Yup, that's your girl." He couldn't get over the transformation of his alpaca.

I'm pleased that she is now a farm favorite on their property. She is full of kisses and really enjoys children. When their grandchildren visit, Pistachio is the alpaca they want to hang out with, giving her carrots and getting kisses. ▒

# The Crows of September 11<sup>th</sup>

I woke up to a huge racket outside my bedroom window. Crows were cawing like mad. It was a little after 5:30 am. It was so loud that I got up to look out my window to see what was going on. I became anxious that maybe an earthquake or some disaster was going to happen because I had never seen or heard such a chaotic noise from birds before. I looked outside the window and saw so many birds swirling in the sky across the street from my house. I felt chills running up and down my spine. Their caws were unsettling. I stood at my window looking out trying to see if there was some clue as to what was making these birds flying around in a craze and making such a fuss. At such an early hour, there were no people outside. It was all quiet except for the crows.

As I watched them, I noticed that their flight patterns didn't seem random and chaotic as I had initially thought. Some birds seemed to be attacking each other and flying straight at each other. It was like an aerial dog fight with fighter aircraft going after each other. But after watching them for several minutes, I saw that their attacks were not real. They missed each other and now it looked more like watching the Blue Angels perform their aerial dance maneuvers done with such precision. I was fascinated by the acrobatic aerodynamics going on outside my bedroom. I kept looking around to see if any human was out and about, but there was no sign of anyone.

I know how animals can sense earthquakes, so I turned on the TV to see if anything was going on in the news I should be aware of. I turned my set on and went back to the window to watch.

As I further watched the birds, I could see that they were flying at each other from all four directions of the compass. After the aerial maneuvers, one set of birds would fly to one of the four directions of the compass and land. As they landed, a bird seemingly resting or waiting its turn to do its maneuver would take off and fly towards the center point that happened to be right across the street in front of my bedroom window.

I wasn't paying attention to the TV and had been standing there for some time concentrating on watching the birds, when I finally heard what the newscaster was saying. They were talking about the anniversary of the twin towers being hit by the airplanes on September 11th. I was reminded that it was the one year anniversary of the September 11th attack. The newscaster was describing the ceremony. A dignitary would hit a gong at the exact time each airplane hit one of the towers and for the aircrafts that crashed in Pennsylvania and the Pentagon. I continued to watch the birds and listen to the news. It was surreal watching these birds fly their ritual patterns. I observed the birds do their flights and maneuvers until the last gong was struck. As soon as that last gong rang representing the last plane crash, the birds suddenly stopped their maneuvers and stopped cawing and it became eerily quiet outside. The timing was exact. A moment of silence was held in remembrance for those souls lost during the attack. The silence on the TV was happening simultaneously to the silence outside my bedroom window. It was both unnerving and numinous. I watched for a few minutes more to see if the birds would start up again but they didn't. I have never seen birds do anything like that before, nor have I seen it since. I have no idea why they chose to fly like that outside my bedroom window on that day. I had not lost anyone in the towers although it affected me like the rest of the country with such sadness and anger. But why me to see this special flight or ritual of the birds on this memorable day? I can't answer that, but it was a moment I will never forget. ▧

# Sargon

Sargon was an oxymoron of an alpaca. He was an extrovert which is not how you'd define an alpaca. He preferred people to alpacas and the bigger the crowd, the more he liked it. He was a total ham, loving to perform in front of people. During public events or tours on the farm, I would halter Sargon and lead him out to meet the public. I'd swear he would pose for pictures. Kids were his favorites by far. He was the smartest alpaca too. I could train him to do just about anything I could think of. I was teaching him dance steps and my goal was to find just the right music and song and do a simple choreography for him to dance to. Now that

*Sargon was quite the entertainer.*

would be a real show stopper. He was such a character. I adored him. I could not wait to get him to my own farm and have him be my ambassador.

Like the saying goes, best laid plans. Unfortunately, this plan was sadly not meant to be. Just before I was set to have my alpacas transported to my new farm, Sargon took sick. I had already moved to Oregon and I felt such guilt not being with him when he needed me. He was my best buddy. So many friends did their best to fill in for me and I did distant energy work on him, sent down homeopathy, and the vet did what she could too. But, nothing worked and he passed away before he could join me on our beautiful farm. His death put such a pall on what I envisioned for us on our farm. Sargon played such a big role in that vision.

The rest of my herd had arrived only days before Sargon's passing. I went out to take care of my evening chores with such a heavy heart the day he died. It was a cool evening but unlike many November days in Oregon, there was a little sunshine sneaking through the clouds. I was starting my evening chores of feeding and bringing in the alpacas but was stopped from my routine by the antics of my alpacas. They started to race around my big 2-acre back field. They were pronking which looks like skipping. Alpacas run like this when they are happy. Normally, it is the babies that do the pronking run, but this evening, the adult females, led by my beautiful gray Huacaya, Misty Morning, were racing about along with the cria. They ran out to the back and then all the way to the barn. They stopped, turned and repeated their paths back and forth making several laps. What followed was to become one of the most memorable and moving experiences I've had since owning alpacas.

## Alpacas Don't Do That

The alpacas stopped racing back and forth. Instead, they changed course and started to race in a large circle, pronking counter-clockwise. They ran their circle a few times around before stopping. They were spread out when they stopped, remaining in the circle. They turned and all faced towards the center of their large circle. Then Misty bowed her head nearly touching her nose to the ground. She stepped away from the circle and went back to grazing. One by one, each followed Misty's lead repeating what she had done, bowing their heads and then walking away.

Tears came freely as I watched this ritual. The feeling of such love entered my mind and spirit. I was witnessing such a touching act. I knew they were doing their "dance" for Sargon and maybe it was for me too. It reminded me of the crows on the anniversary of September 11th. Do animals ritualize when they experience a loss too? I don't know the answer to that, but I do believe with all my heart, my Sargon was in the middle of that circle, receiving the respect and honor the other alpacas were bestowing upon him. In that moment, I knew that I was in the right place with my alpacas and that no matter how hard this life was going to be with them, the choice was right making the move to my farm and having these animals in my life. I couldn't imagine my life without Sargon in it. Despite the pain of losing him, I would rather experience the pain of loss than not having him in my life at all. The joy of knowing him and having my time with Sargon far outweighed the pain of loss. I wished he could have been in my life a lot longer and had joined us on our farm, but I would never have given up our time together for anything. ❁

# Baby Jackson

Although this book is about my experiences with animals, I am including my experience with Baby Jackson. I do not do much energy work on humans. I prefer to work with animals, but when my oldest sister, Sally, emailed me requesting I send some energy to her friends who recently had a baby who was ill, I said I would do what I could. My sister and her friends live in Canada and I was in California at the time. The only thing I could do was perform distance energy work. I wasn't sure if I would be overly effective not knowing or even having met my sister's friends before, but I would try.

I sat in my favorite chair and closed my eyes asking to reach Baby Jackson. I had no pictures of him which I usually like to have when doing distance work. If I can have a visual, it seems to help me "lock on" to the animal or person better. If I have never met them before, I only have my imagination to picture them.

I found myself immediately going into a trance. I soon saw pictures in my mind of spirits around a baby. I was worried about these spirits. They didn't seem to be helping the baby get better, but wanting to take him to the "other side." I got the feeling the baby had passed and felt sad. But instead of assuming, I asked if he had passed and got the answer "no." I was surprised because I kept seeing those spirits. I asked again to make sure and received "no" as the answer again. I started to do energy sending him gentle, healing white light. I was still worried because if he hadn't passed away, he was very seriously sick and close to death. I then saw a female spirit that felt like she was a healer. She shooed the other spirits away. I pictured her helping direct the energy to Baby Jackson.

I came out of that energy session feeling worried. I rarely see images when I do energy work. I may see a brief image or have a word placed in my head as a thought or feeling but this was very dramatic and distinct imagery. I conveyed what I saw to Sally. The next day, she hadn't heard much news other than he had to be airlifted to Calgary to the Children's Hospital, but no word on Baby Jackson's status. She asked if I would do more energy on him. Of course I would.

I sat down in my chair again that evening and immediately entered into a trance. I didn't see any spirits but I had a very odd physical reaction. Every time I took a breath, it felt as if my lungs hesitated in taking in the oxygen and then it felt as if they were being forced to expand to get air in. With every breath, my lungs worked oddly. It was a bit uncomfortable. I took it as a sign that I was tapped into Baby Jackson and that energy needed to go to his lungs. I focused on his lungs and sent white light and gentle energy there. My lungs relaxed and began working normally again. I didn't see any spirits this time, but still felt he was a very sick little boy. I emailed Sally to let her know about this energy session.

That night, I had a terrible nightmare. I dreamt I was in the car with an old family friend. She had passed away about a year earlier. She had been one of my mom's best friends. In my dream, she was driving the car and she suddenly had a stroke. We were heading off the road and I reached for the steering wheel to get us back on the road. As we were about to crash, I woke up. I thought what an odd dream.

Mrs. Schallheim had died of cancer, not a stroke, so I didn't understand why I was dreaming of her having a stroke.

I got up and was mulling over my dream as I fixed my breakfast. I booted up computer to check my email which was my normal routine. I had an email from Sally. I opened it first to see if there was news of Baby Jackson. She had heard from the family and the details of his illness. For days, all my sister and I knew was that Baby Jackson was very sick, but we didn't know what was causing his serious illness that forced him to be so far from home in a special hospital.

The email said that Baby Jackson had a serious heart issue. The first day I had done energy on him and saw all those spirits, his heart had stopped and they had to revive him. His lungs weren't working right and he couldn't handle breathing on his own. As a result, Baby Jackson was placed on a ventilator. This validated my feelings of why my lungs felt as if they were being forced to expand to get the oxygen into them. The final note of his status said he had suffered a stroke while they were working on reviving him. My dream made sense now. All the experiences I had while doing energy work on Baby Jackson were explained, but I wasn't aware of any of them when I was performing the energy work. It showed me how powerful sending positive, white light energy is to someone who is sick. It is non-invasive and supports the efforts of the doctors and nurses doing their work. Certainly, the tremendous skill and technology was the reason for Baby Jackson surviving but I believe it also helped him during those moments of crisis to receive a little added energy to help him survive. If I wasn't a full believer of energy work before this experience, I was convinced afterwards and became more confident in my intuitive abilities. The best news is that Baby Jackson recovered. ❖

# Makeanu's Mojo

Makeanu is an alpaca herdsire owned by Alison, a good friend of mine. He was being boarded in Southern California while my friend built her farm. While he was in a large herd of males, he experienced a traumatic event that left him constantly anxious. Days, weeks and months passed and Makeanu remained very upset. Alison called me to discuss his state of anxiety. I offered to have him come to my place so I could work with him. I had only a few male alpacas and

*Big Mak loves his carrots.*

being in a smaller environment might help him regain his machismo.

Makeanu came up to Oregon on the next transport available. He is a larger than average alpaca. He weighed over 225 pounds when he arrived on my farm. That is rather big considering even larger males rarely tip the scale at more than 200 pounds. I was fond of Makeanu because I had used him as a stud. He was Opus' father. Before the incident, Mak was reserved but easy going. He wasn't a male that fought unless he was pushed. Since he was so large, most males knew better than challenge him.

When Mak arrived, he was extremely skittish and passive. He jumped even when I moved slowly around him as I raked poop. I talked to him when I raked and offered him goodies, but he wouldn't come close to me. Even at suppertime when I would feed their favorite pellets, he was reluctant to come into the barn area where the males eat. He waited until I left before coming to his bowl. This went on for months and I never tried to do more than offer him treats occasionally.

Eventually, Mak would take pellets from my hands. Then he learned to take carrots. Once he became brave enough to try a carrot, he became hooked. If carrots were offered, he became very piggish and didn't want to let any of the others have any. He became comfortable with our routine and after the other males challenged him a couple of times, he learned that if he chest butted one of them, they flew back several feet and stayed far away. None of my males could come close to challenging Mak. He was so much stronger and bigger than my boys.

About six months passed and Mak was comfortable coming into the barn stall for pellets with me in there. If another male got there first, he would just look at him out of the corner of his eye and the other boys would back off to give Mak his pick of bowls. If it was Baloo being given the eye, he would squeal with displeasure, but instantly give up his bowl to Mak. The other boys were also too afraid to eat out of their bowls near Mak, so I took to feeding them outside the stall so all of them would get to have their pellets. I was pleased to see Mak getting his mojo back. I noticed that the rest of the herd started to look to Mak as their leader. It was not just the males that saw him as the lead. If the females alarmed, Mak would grow very tall and statuesque, keeping an eye on the herd. He had become a strong presence and he kept the alpacas calm. There was very little fighting amongst the males. His dominance was secure and they had no desire to challenge him.

Mak was doing really well and had become self-assured when I noticed he was laying down more and something seemed off. I wasn't sure what wasn't right, but Mak just didn't seem himself. I observed him closely as I raked. His eyes didn't seem as bright and he was moving his mouth oddly like maybe it hurt. I caught him and examined him to see if I could see if he had an injury in his mouth. I didn't see anything. I suggested to Alison that I have the vet examine him after watching him for a day or two. He wasn't eating much at all and looking punier by the day. I was getting very worried about him. The vet examined him but couldn't find anything wrong with his mouth. He told me to call him if things didn't improve.

The next morning when I went out to check on Mak, I knew he was really sick. I called Alison and suggested we get him up to Oregon State University Veterinary hospital. I called my vet to get the approval and referral to take him in. I loaded him in my car and rushed him there.

Makeanu was so sweet at the hospital. I held his lead while they examined him. Normally he would not let anyone touch him without being restrained in a chute, but he stood passively as they listened to his heart and lungs and checked inside his mouth. He was too weak to resist. They told me they would need to put an IV in him because he was dehydrated. I knew that would boost his energy to get fluids in him as quickly as possible. They were going to keep him overnight and there was nothing more I could do for him. I gave him a kiss and told him mentally that he was in good hands and that I would be reaching out to him with energy. I told him I loved him and to be strong. With tears in my eyes, I left him at the hospital. Later, the doctors told me that I had gotten Mak to the hospital just in time. Another hour delay and he might not have made it.

I sent Mak energy every day. They ran test after test trying to find the cause of his illness. I would feel Mak in my mind and I knew to stop what I was doing to send him energy and tell him I would come and get him as soon as he was well enough. He spent the week at the hospital and no diagnosis was determined, but he was eating and drinking on his own. He just needed time to regain his strength. I was so happy when I got the call that Mak was ready to come back to my farm. I ran right up to get him. He was still weak and he had lost so much weight. He was less than 170 pounds now. He had lost more than 50 pounds since he arrived on my farm!

I didn't want to put Mak back in with the adult males. I was worried they would sense his weakness and take advantage of it. Males will challenge any new males coming into their pasture. They consider a male new to the pasture even if they are gone only five minutes! I didn't want Mak to have to fight for his pecking order so soon after being released from the hospital. I had a new pasture of weanling males and even though I didn't know how it would work out I didn't think any of them would challenge Mak. I put him in with them and that worked very nicely. They left Mak alone and would even go into a submissive posture with their tails up in the air and neck hunched down as they tried to make themselves look like little cria if they walked near him. Mak took a couple of months to recuperate, but slowly he regained his strength. I saw his demeanor change and he showed more confidence again. It was time to put him back with the bigger males.

Baloo would posture at Mak from the safety of his side of the fence while Mak was recovering in the younger boy pasture. When I put Mak back in with Baloo, Clyde, and Mowgli, Baloo didn't realize that the fence protecting him was gone and he postured at Mak like he was a tough guy. I hadn't gotten the gate closed yet and Mak tore after Baloo. He had been "teased" over the fence for weeks and months and Mak was ready to teach Baloo a lesson. I had to laugh as Baloo ran around my back field screaming for dear life with Mak chasing after him. But, the tears in my eyes were because Big Mak was back!

One of my proudest and happiest moments since owning my own farm was when I sent Mak home to Alison and his own farm. I knew I was sending back a male that I helped to recover from his traumatic experiences. I was also sad to see him go because he had become the head of my herd. It made me feel good that I was able to pay back a little what these alpacas have done for me. Like Mak, I had lost my way and confidence from all of my traumatic life experiences.

My life with alpacas has not been an easy one. It has been sometimes filled with trauma, but my animal encounters have provided me tools to better handle those hard times. When I first got my alpacas, the running joke was "Alpacas don't do that." I would reply, "They do now!" I could also say the same thing about me. Before having alpacas, Cindy Myers would never have had the courage to pull up stakes and move to a farm. I wouldn't have ever admitted that I have the ability to do energy work and have mental communications with animals either. I would have led a very safe and predictive life.

Farm life is a great teacher regarding the cycle of life. There is no fairy tale happily ever after. It is such a mix of joy and sadness, intense grief filled with the most touching moments, tears and laughter, and they can happen simultaneously. It is a life tapestry of events and emotions. That white board that had been wiped clean after the fire is pretty full again, because my alpacas have become my life's passion and taught me to think beyond my limits. ▓

*About the author*

*Cindy Myers owns and operates her own farm, Alpacas at Hum Sweet Hum. She has an M.A. in Counseling Psychology with an emphasis in Depth Psychology from Pacifica Graduate Institute and earned a B.S. in Aerospace Engineering from San Diego State University. She also has level II certification in Reiki and is a Healing Touch Practitioner. She is certified in TAGTEACH and teaches workshops in Positive Reinforcement Techniques. She takes great care breeding high quality alpacas and caring for her herd. Her passions include writing, spinning her alpacas' fiber, and training her three dogs, Wiley, Moose, and Harper.*

Made in the USA
Lexington, KY
26 September 2013